New York
Sweets

PHOTOGRAPHY BY *Battman*

DISTRIBUTED IN THE UNITED STATES BY BATTMAN STUDIOS
NEW YORK, NEW YORK

PUBLISHED BY BATTMAN STUDIOS
TEXT AND PHOTOGRAPHS © 2005 BY BATTMAN
ALL RIGHTS RESERVED. PRINTED IN CHINA

ISBN 0-933477-25-2

WWW.BATTMANSTUDIOS.COM

BOOK DESIGN BY LISA SRAGG, EN MODA DESIGN, NEW YORK
ADDITIONAL GRAPHICS BY CYNTHIA MALARAN
RECIPE EDITORS: PATRICIA MCCORMICK, ANDREA TUTUNJIAN, CARA TANNENBAUM

FRONT COVER PHOTOGRAPH: THE MODERN, NEW YORK
BACK COVER PHOTOGRAPH: THE RIVER CAFE, NEW YORK

RESTAURANTS AND CHEFS

Forward

Alan Batt is affectionately called "Battman" by all his friends and colleagues as a play on his name. But, the name really stuck for another reason. Battman is able to assemble the most unpredictable and varied group of chefs for his books of food photography. Through his supersensitive "radar", his intuition and his para-physical talents, he somehow brings out the most from each of us. Just as the fictional Batman draws solutions to crimes by reductive logic and by involving his protégé Robin, this Battman as food photographer reveals the magic of a beautifully prepared and plated dish.

The great chef Roger Vergé once told me that a chef who has to think about his work is not a master. An accomplished painter also does his work without over analyzing it. Battman photographs from the gut as well. The chef's dish has been barely placed in front of him and he is finished capturing it for all to see and sense.

Battman's process does not produce a sloppy first impression or a slap-dash attitude. His instinct is for color, texture, symmetry, structure, dimension, geometry, depth, focus and feeling. And, the image all comes together in perfect sync. His ability is also experiential. Photography is not what he does; it is who he is. Just as the best golfer or archer or tennis player considers the club or the bow or the racket as an extension of the arm, Battman's lens is another natural eye.

Looking at our desires and ourselves from a few steps removed can teach us a great deal. Looking at our favorite desserts through photography can teach us what makes us salivate, what turns us on, what makes us really tick. We are certain that the reality of a dessert must always be more appealing than a version of it on paper, but it's an amazing feat to deliver an image that is

perfected and reorganized, one that titillates and tantalizes and teases. Battman through his photography satisfies the viewer intellectually and provides a different level of immediate gratification.

This book of dessert photos displays the incredible talent and diversity of dessert chefs and the different creations they invent and produce to please and entertain their public.

Within are desserts that are easily recognizable and that you want to dive right into with your fork or spoon. Some appear as weightless hummingbirds floating above the plate – happily defying the Laws of Newton and of common sense. Some of these sweet masters have used a familiar cake or cookie to lure in their prey and then they unexpectedly switch out the reward with a surprise element or ingredient. There are creations that entice with abundant, sheer, decadent self-indulgence as their riveting hook and this "take-no-prisoners" approach makes for spectacular photos and desserts! Full-blown exoticism can be found here, too, in the guise of over-the-top, thirty-two ingredient extravaganzas culled from Asia Minor, harvested only on the night of the full moon, Mercury-rising type of dessert. Viewing these concoctions might replace an overseas trip. Battman's interpretive desserts provide something for everyone.

Your inner child and your inner glutton will enjoy this book. There is much nuance and humor in the dishes depicted here as befits a book about this most illogical course – the beloved dessert course. It's the one that comes when the diner is no longer hungry, has spent too much time and money at table, has possibly over-imbibed and

may have even talked too much. Then, you're offered one more course, that course has no claim to any nutritional, social or salubrious redeeming value. It is "de trop" by every calculation and to every reasonable mind, but we want it anyway. Savory courses are food for the body and mind. Dessert is food for the soul. Dessert is eating for pure pleasure. That is enough, we've earned it.

Where do your thoughts lead you when they begin their journey on a photo of molten chocolate cake or some such temptation? Perhaps to nirvana, perhaps to the refrigerator. In any case, the trip is not boring and that is the real reason to turn these pages.

The icing on this cake of a book is that like food professionals themselves, it will give in a generous way to others. Ten percent of the proceeds of the sales of the book will go to support "The Children's Storefront", an independent school in Harlem located on 129th Street. The pre-to 8th grade school, which offers a safe haven for children to engage in a variety of educational activities, was started in 1966 and is accredited by the New York State Association of Independent Schools. It is a miraculous success story and one of those hope-fulfilling places hugely important for children who have few advantages. Go to their wonderful website to learn more about them, www.thechildrensstorefront.org, and enjoy the terrific music there while you savor desserts.

BILL YOSSES | EXECUTIVE CHEF | JOSEPHS CITARELLA

Strawberry Cannelloni

Cannelloni
12 sheets gelatin
1 quart strawberry puree
¾ cup sugar

1. Place gelatin in a bowl of ice cold water, set aside to soften.
2. In a sauce pan, combine the strawberry puree and the sugar and bring to a simmer over medium heat.
3. Squeeze excess water out of softened gelatin and dissolve the soft gelatin in the hot puree. Pass through a fine mesh strainer.
4. Pour the mixture in a small square container and freeze.

Cream Filling
6 gelatin leaves
3 cups heavy cream, divided
½ cup sugar
3 vanilla beans, split and scraped
2 lbs. 8 oz. crème fraiche

1. Place gelatin in a bowl of ice cold water, set aside to soften.
2. In a saucepan, combine half of the heavy cream with the sugar and vanilla beans and bring to a simmer over medium heat.
3. Squeeze excess water out of softened gelatin and dissolve the soft gelatin in cream mixture.
4. Combine the hot mixture with the remaining heavy cream and crème fraiche. Pass through a fine mesh strainer.
5. Chill mixture until the gelatin sets.

BLUE HILL
AT STONE BARNS

PASTRY CHEF
Michael Moorhouse

Assembly
1. In a bowl of a standing mixer, fitted with the paddle attachment, beat the cream mixture until soft.
2. Fill a pastry bag, fitted with a ¼" plain tip with the cream mixture.
3. Unmold the strawberry puree and slice paper thin on a rotary slicer or a mandolin.
4. Line up squares of frozen strawberry sheets and pipe a cylinder of cream mixture onto edge closest to you.
5. Working quickly, roll sheets around cream and transfer to a clean plate or a baking sheet.
6. Serve immediately with sorbet or reserve covered in the refrigerator.
7. Use within 24 hours.

YUZU POT D'CRÈME

SERVES 8

YUZU CURD

1 cup yuzu (available in
specialty Japanese markets)

12 egg yolks

2 cups sugar

2 sticks unsalted butter

3 sheets gelatin, softened in
ice cold water

1. Using a double boiler over medium high heat, combine ¾ cup
   of the yuzu juice, egg yolks, and sugar.
2. Whisk continuously until thick and pale yellow.
3. Remove the yuzu and egg yolk mixture from the heat and
   whisk in the butter.
4. Heat the remaining ¼ cup of yuzu juice over medium heat in
   a non-reactive saucepot and add the softened gelatin.
5. Remove from the heat and stir until the gelatin is dissolved.
6. Stir the dissolved gelatin mixture into the egg mixture.

Note – the recipe can be made up to this point and stored in the refrigerator for up to three days.

POPPY SEED PUREE

¾ cup poppy seeds

1 cup sugar

1 ½ cups mineral or
filtered water

1. Combine all ingredients in a heavy bottomed saucepan and cook over
   medium low heat.
2. Allow the syrup to simmer for approximately 45 minutes, or until the
   poppy seeds turn from grey to black. During this period you may need
   to add more water as it evaporates.
3. While it is still hot, puree in the pot with a hand held blender. The poppy
   seeds should break down. If not, just continue cooking for another ten
   minutes and puree again.
4. Allow to cool. If the mixture becomes too thick after cooling, just add a
   little water and stir until you get a maple syrup like consistency

TO FINISH THE MOUSSE

1 quart heavy cream

¼ cup confectioners' sugar

1. Combine the cream and sugar in a chilled mixing bowl or mixer.
2. Slowly whisk the cream to soft to medium peaks. The cream should
   just begin to hold its shape.
3. Fold cream into the curd a little bit at a time until well incorporated.

Note – I like the sharp, sour flavor of the yuzu. Therefore, I tend to hold back on the cream. Add according to your taste.

PHYLLO CUPS

6 phyllo sheets

6 – 4 ounce ramekins

2 tablespoons butter or
spray oil

1. Preheat your oven to 350º.
2. Cut each phyllo sheet into 4 equal pieces, for a total of 24 squares.
3. Take one square and lightly coat with butter or oil. Keep the remaining squares
   covered with a slightly moist kitchen towel to prevent them from drying out.
4. Place another square on top. Continue until you have four squares. Repeat 5
   more times until you have a total of six squares that are four layers thick.
5. Take the six ramekins upside down and place them on a cookie sheet.
6. Spray or coat the outside with butter or oil.
7. Loosely drape one phyllo square over each ramekin.
8. Bake approximately 15 minutes, until golden brown.

EXECUTIVE CHEF
Jake Klein

ASSEMBLY

1 pint strawberries

1. Take a spoon full of the poppy seed puree and make horizontal streaks across
   the bottom of the plate.
2. Take one of the phyllo cups and place it in the middle of the plate.
3. Spoon about ¾ cup of yuzu mousse into the cup. Garnish with strawberries.

Note – At the restaurant, we use preserved roses, which can be quite difficult to find.
Diced strawberries would make a perfect alternative.

BREAD PUDDING

3 cups heavy cream

¾ cup sugar, divided

6 egg yolks

¼ cup rum

Pinch of nutmeg

Pinch of cinnamon
1½ lbs. Italian bread with
crust removed
and cut in 1-inch diced pieces

¼ cup raisins

1. In a saucepan, bring cream and half the sugar to a boil over medium heat.
2. Whisk the remaining sugar with egg yolks.
3. While whisking, pour some of the boiling cream over the egg yolks. While whisking, return the egg yolk mixture into the hot cream and continue to cook over low heat until it coats the back of a spoon, approximately 1 minute.
4. Add the rum and strain.
5. Add nutmeg and cinnamon.
6. Sprinkle bread and raisins in a 9" pyrex dish.
7. Pour custard over cut up bread cubes and raisins. Bake at 350º for approximately 30 minutes.

NEGRIL VILLAGE

EXECUTIVE CHEF
Marva Layne

White Chocolate Pinnacle with Vanilla Mousse

THE MODERN

PASTRY CHEF
Marc Aumont

Cones

10 oz. white chocolate, chopped
¼ cup cocoa butter

1. Take pieces of parchment paper and fold them over to make a triangle. Cut in half so you end up with two triangles. Then roll the paper to create the shape of a cone and staple to hold.
2. Temper the white chocolate and the cocoa butter. In a glass bowl or plastic container, heat together in microwave on medium power (50 percent, do not use high power) checking every 15 seconds, stirring to evenly disperse heat, for no more than a total of 2 minutes or less. You don't want to fully melt the chocolate in the microwave.
3. Once the chocolate becomes shiny, do not continue to microwave (it won't look melted). Remove from the microwave and stir for 1 minute to complete the melting process and stabilize the temperature.
4. Pour into cones and then invert on a wire rack allowing excess chocolate to drip out.
5. Just before they dry, approximately 5 to 10 minutes, lay them on their side.

Mousse

1 cup sugar
6 Tbsp. glucose
1 cup water
1¼ cups condensed milk
Pinch of salt
½ tsp. vanilla extract
2¼ cups heavy cream

1. Boil the sugar, glucose, and ½ cup water together until it turns caramel in color.
2. Carefully add the remaining ½ cup water and bring back to a boil.
3. Remove from flame and cool.
4. Once cool, add condensed milk, salt, and vanilla.
5. In a separate bowl, whip the heavy cream to soft peaks.
6. Take about ½ of the whipped cream and fold it into the caramel mixture.
7. Then take the caramel and fold it into the rest of the whipped cream.
8. Pipe the mousse into the cones. Fill a little higher than the top.
9. Invert onto parchment lined sheet tray and put in freezer overnight.

Balsamic Sauce

1¼ cups sugar
9 oz. water
1 cup balsamic vinegar
½ pint raspberries
½ pint blackberries

1. Heat sugar in a pot over a medium-high heat, stirring ever so slightly to assist the melting process and cook until it turns medium golden in color.
2. Carefully add the water and vinegar and cook over a medium flame until thick enough to coat the back of a spoon.
3. Put the raspberries and blackberries in the pot and carefully stir until coated.
4. Remove from flame and chill.

Assembly

1. Peel paper from cone and place on a plate.
2. Decorate with berries and sauce.

MILLE FEUILLE

SERVES 12

MILK CHOCOLATE BISCUIT
¼ cup cake flour
2 ½ Tbsp. granulated sugar
9 Tbsp. unsalted butter, softened
5 ½ oz. milk chocolate, melted
4 large eggs, separated
2 Tbsp. invert sugar (usually found in jars in cake decorating supply shops)
2 Tbsp. granulated sugar

1. Preheat oven to 400°.
2. Combine and sift flour and 2 tablespoons of sugar. Reserve.
3. In a medium size bowl, thoroughly incorporate butter into melted chocolate. Stir in egg yolks and invert sugar.
4. Meanwhile, begin whipping egg whites, adding 2 tablespoons of sugar, to soft peaks.
5. Fold in sifted cake flour, followed by the milk chocolate base.
6. Bake in a prepared 9 x 9 inch square pan or baking dish for 13 to 18 minutes. Allow to cool. Store under refrigeration.
7. Cut into rectangles measuring 1" by 3" and reserve for assembly.

PRALINE CREAM
3 oz. heavy cream
⅔ cup (5 oz). praline paste

1. In a small saucepan, heat cream just until warm.
2. Place praline paste in the bowl of an electric stand mixer. Using the paddle attachment, slowly incorporate the cream, mixing until completely emulsified.

MILK CHOCOLATE CREAM
1 cup heavy cream
5 oz. milk chocolate, chopped

1. In a small saucepan, bring cream to a boil over high heat.
2. Place chocolate in a bowl and slowly incorporate hot cream into the chocolate, stirring until smooth.
3. Cover, chill and allow to rest for several hours.
4. In an electric stand mixer, whip until stiff.
5. Transfer to a pastry bag fitted with a large, straight tip. Reserve.

PRALINE FEUILLETINE
3 oz. milk chocolate, melted
5 oz. (⅔ cup) praline paste
5 oz. (⅔ cup) feuilletine
(can be found in specialty stores)

1. In a large bowl, combine melted chocolate and praline paste.
2. Stir in feuilletine until completely combined.
3. Transfer to a silpat or parchment-lined surface. Place a second liner on top and roll to a ¼" thickness with a rolling pin. Chill.
4. Remove from refrigeration and cut into rectangles measuring 1" by 3". Reserve.

PEDRO XIMENEZ SOAKED PRUNES
¾ cup prunes, pitted and chopped
½ cup sherry, preferably a sweeter Pedro Ximenez style

1. Combine prunes and sherry in a small, lidded container and allow to soak up to 24 hours. Reserve.

ASSEMBLY
36 Ecuadorian chocolate plaquettes, 3½" by 4"
Maldon sea salt

1. Onto each serving plate, place 1 chocolate plaquette, topping each with a rectangle of the biscuit.
2. Follow the biscuit with a second plaquette and a rectangle of feuilletine.
3. Pipe 2 lines of the milk chocolate cream onto the feuilletine, finishing the presentaton with a final chocolate plaquette.
4. Sauce the plate with the praline cream and prunes.
5. Sprinkle with a few grains of Maldon sea salt.
6. Serve immediately.

Le Bernardin

PASTRY CHEF
Michael Laiskonis

LEMON MERINGUE TART WITH LEMONGRASS BLUEBERRY SAUCE AND WHIPPED CREAM

MAKES 36 INDIVIDUAL TARTS

TART
6 cups flour
8 sticks butter
2 cups sugar
3 eggs

1. Cream butter and sugar. Add flour and then eggs. Chill overnight.
2. Roll dough to ⅛" thick and mold into individual 2½" tart shells. Let sit in the refrigerator for a few hours.
3. Remove from refrigerator and cover with parchment paper. Place beans on top to weigh down the parchment paper and help keep the tarts flat.
4. Bake at 375° for 8 to 10 minutes.

SWISS MERINGUE
7 egg whites
1 box superfine sugar

1. Heat egg whites until just barely warm to the touch (100°) in a double boiler, while whisking gently.
2. In a kitchen aid or with a hand mixer, whip egg whites and sugar to stiff peaks.
3. Place meringue in a star-tipped pastry bag.

LEMON FILLING
1⅓ cups lemon and lime juice
¾ cup plus 1 Tbsp. sugar
2 sticks plus 1 Tbsp. butter
7 egg yolks
¾ cup plus 1 Tbsp. sugar
6 eggs

1. Bring juice, sugar, and butter to a rolling boil.
2. Whisk yolks and second sugar together.
3. Lower heat and add egg yolks/sugar mixture.
4. Whisk constantly while bringing it back to a boil.
5. Strain into a clean bowl and chill.

LEMONGRASS BLUEBERRY SAUCE
4½ pints blueberries
3 cups sugar
6 stalks lemongrass (ethnic section of market)
6 sprigs lemon thyme
1 cup lemon juice
6 cinnamon sticks
½ tsp. ground cloves

1. Bring all ingredients to a boil.
2. Remove cinnamon sticks
3. Puree in a food processor or blender in batches.
4. Strain and chill.

ASSEMBLY
1. Pipe or spoon the lemon filling neatly into the tart shells.
2. Let chill in the refrigerator.
3. Pipe the meringue on top of the tarts.
4. Lightly burn under a broiler briefly, or use a hand torch.
5. Use lemongrass blueberry sauce to decorate the plate.

Allen Street Bakery

PASTRY CHEF
Morgan Larsson

CARAMELIZED PEAR WITH POUND CAKE

CARAMEL
1 cup water
2 cups sugar
½ cup water

1. Pour the 1 cup of water and the sugar into a heavy-bottomed pan.
2. Place on high heat and boil until sugar starts to color, approximately 10 minutes. Allow the caramel to turn amber and then turn the heat down under the pan.
3. Add the ½ cup of water slowly as the caramel will splash. Continue to cook for 1 minute.

POACHED PEARS
4 bosc pears
½ cup sugar
1 cup water
Prepared caramel

1. Peel the pears, following the shape of the pear. Core out the pear from the bottom, using a melon baller.
2. Take the caramel in the pan and add sugar and water.
3. Submerge the pears in the liquid and cover with a circle of parchment paper.
4. Bring liquid to a boil and then turn down to a simmer for 30 minutes, occasionally rotating the pears.

CARAMEL PASSION SAUCE
1 cup passion fruit juice
1 cup sugar
1 cup water

1. Boil sugar and water to a dark amber color.
2. Carefully add passion fruit juice and continue to boil for 1 minute. Cool.
3. Once cold, pour this over the pear and along the plate to serve

POUND CAKE
4 oz. butter, softened
½ cup sugar
2 eggs, room temperature
½ cup all purpose flour
¼ tsp. baking soda
1 Tbsp. cocoa powder

1. In a mixer, beat butter and sugar until pale. Add eggs and continue to beat until light and fluffy, scraping down the sides at least once.
2. Add flour and baking powder and pulse. Once mixed, beat until satin gloss texture appears.
3. Separate ¼ of the mix and add the cocoa powder to it by hand.
4. Place 4" rings on parchment lined sheet pan with a non-stick spray. Spray the rings before filling.
5. With a piping bag and small plain tip, pipe the chocolate mix in small dots against the edge of the ring (7 in each ring).
6. Then fill the ring in with the white cake mix using a piping bag so as not to disturb the chocolate mix around the edge.
7. Bake at 325º for 20 to 25 minutes.

OATMEAL CRISP
⅛ cup almonds, toasted and cooled
2 Tbsp. butter
2 Tbsp. all purpose flour
⅛ cup dark brown sugar
¼ cup quick oats
½ tsp. ground cinnamon
½ tsp. ground ginger

1. Combine all ingredients in a food processor. Pulse the mix together. Do not mix too much. You don't want it too fine.
2. Spread the mixture out on a sheet pan and bake at 350º until golden brown, 5 to 7 minutes.
3. This is used under the ice cream to hold it in place and give a crisp texture.

PASSION SORBET
2 cups passion fruit juice
1½ cups simple syrup

1. Simply mix together and freeze in an ice cream machine.

VANILLA ICE CREAM
10 egg yolks
¾ cup sugar
1 qt. half and half
1 vanilla bean, split

1. Whisk together the egg yolks and sugar.
2. Put half and half and vanilla bean in a saucepan to boil.
3. Take ½ of it and pour it in with the egg yolks while whisking constantly. Then return it all to the pot and cook until it thickens enough to coat the back of a spoon.
4. Remove from heat and strain through a fine strainer into a clean bowl.
5. Cool down and run in an ice cream machine.
6. The vanilla ice cream will be combined with the passion fruit sorbet to make a ribbon effect. This can be done by running them through the ice cream machine together for a turn or two.

21

PASTRY CHEF
Paul Nolan

OVEN ROASTED STRAWBERRY, BLACK SESAME MACAROON, ALMOND SOUP, AND ROSE PETALS

OVEN ROASTED STRAWBERRY
12 strawberries
1 cup sugar
Pinch of peppercorn
1 Tbsp. olive oil
1 Tbsp. unsalted butter

1. Rinse and hull the strawberries.
2. In a bowl, toss the strawberries in sugar and peppercorn.
3. Heat the olive oil and butter in a small pan over high heat and sear the strawberries.
4. To finish, place strawberries on a pan and bake in a 350º oven for approximately 8 minutes.

CANDIED ROSE PETALS
1 rose (petals only)
2 egg whites
1 cup sugar

1. Dip each petal in the egg whites, lightly beaten and cover in sugar.
2. Lay them flat on a parchment paper-lined sheet pan and allow to dry at room temperature over night.

ALMOND SOUP
2 cups milk
¾ cup almond flour
½ cup almond cream (recipe below)

1. In a saucepan over medium heat, bring the milk and almond flour to a boil, whisking often.
2. Set aside for 15 minutes and then strain through a fine mesh strainer.
3. Using a hand held blender, puree a ½ cup of the almond cream into the milk.

ALMOND CREAM
½ cup unsalted butter, softened
½ cup almond powder
½ cup sugar
1 egg
1 egg yolk
3 Tbsp. calvados

1. In a standing mixer fitted with a paddle attachment, cream the butter and almond powder together until light.
2. Beat in the sugar.
3. Add the egg and then the yolk, scraping the bowl down between each addition.
4. Mix in the calvados until fully incorporated.

BLACK SESAME MACAROON
1 cup almond powder
2 cup confectioners' sugar, divided
3 large egg whites
½ tsp. egg white powder
Black sesame seeds

1. Sift the almond powder and half the confectioners' sugar together.
2. In a bowl of a standing mixer, whisk the egg whites with the remaining confectioners' sugar, and egg white powder until stiff peaks form.
3. Fold almond sugar mixture into the whites in three stages until incorporated.
4. Using a pastry bag fitted with a ½" plain tip, pipe the mixture into 2" diameter circles on parchment paper-lined sheet pan, sprinkle with sesame seeds and let rest for 15 to 20 minutes to form a "skin".
5. Bake at 225º until done – rotating every 4 minutes. They should be hard and dry with little to no color.

ASSEMBLY
Saba, to garnish
Microthyme, to garnish
Chocolate cigarettes, to garnish

1. On a rectangular white plate, place a macaroon in the center. Top with 3 strawberries and then chocolate cigarettes.
2. Place a trail of almond soup foam next to the macaroon.
3. On the left hand side of the plate, draw an X with the saba from the top end to the bottom end, then draw another line straight down the center of the X.
4. Place a rose petal on each top end of the line towards the edge.
5. Garnish the top right corner of the plate with a line of microthyme.

pluton

EXECUTIVE CHEF / OWNER
Jacky Pluton

CHICAGO

DECONSTRUCTED BLACK FOREST CAKE

CHOCOLATE SOUR CREAM CAKE

1 stick unsalted butter, softened at room temperature
1 ½ cups light brown sugar, packed
2 eggs
1 tsp. pure vanilla extract
6 Tbsp. unsweetened cocoa powder
1 ½ tsp. baking soda
¼ tsp. salt
1 ½ cups sifted cake flour
⅔ cup sour cream
¾ cup hot coffee

1. Preheat the oven to 350º.
2. Butter and then line a rectangular sheet cake pan (9 X 13) with parchment paper that extend up the short ends, lengthwise, to use as handles to lift the cake out of the pan.
3. In a mixer fitted with a whisk attachment (or using a hand mixer), cream the butter until smooth. Add the sugar and eggs and mix until fluffy, about 3 minutes. Add the vanilla, cocoa, baking soda and salt and mix until incorporated. Add half of the flour, then half of the sour cream, and mix until incorporated. Repeat with the remaining flour and sour cream. Drizzle in the hot coffee and mix until smooth. The batter will be thin.
4. Pour into the prepared pan and bake until the top is firm to the touch and a toothpick inserted into the center comes out clean, about 35 minutes. Halfway through the baking, quickly rotate the pans in the oven to ensure even baking, but otherwise try not to open the oven.
5. Let cool in the pan. Chill it (even over night) then lift it out of the pan by the paper and cut out round plugs 2-3 inches in diameter of cake with a round pastry cutter or round cookie cutter. Keep wrapped up until ready to serve (they can be frozen at this point)

T R U

EXECUTIVE PASTRY CHEF
Gale Gand

CHICAGO

FUDGE POT

2 oz. best-quality bittersweet chocolate, chopped
2 cups heavy cream
Pinch of salt
3 egg yolks
⅓ cup sugar

1. Heat the oven to 300º.
2. Place the chopped chocolate in a bowl.
3. Combine the cream and salt in a saucepan and bring to a boil over medium-high heat. As soon as it boils, remove from heat and pour over the chocolate, mixing until melted. Put saucepan back on the stove.
4. Whisk the yolks and sugar together in a medium bowl.
5. A little at a time, add all the hot chocolate mixture to the egg mixture, mixing after each addition.
6. Pour back into the saucepan and heat it over medium heat until slightly thickened. The mixture should be thick enough to smoothly coat the back of a wooden spoon. Run your finger down the back of the spoon. When the edges do not blur, the mixture is ready.
7. Pour the mixture into 8 or 10 mini ramekins and place in a hot water bath. The water should come ¾ up the sides of each ramekin.
8. Cover the pan tightly with foil and bake in the center of the oven until almost set but still jiggly in the center, 20 to 30 minutes. (The custard will finish cooking as it cools).
9. Remove from the water bath and let cool 15 minutes.
10. Tightly cover each ramekin with plastic wrap, making sure the plastic does not touch the surface of the custard. Refrigerate at least 2 hours.

CHERRY COMPOTE

1 ½ cups bing or sour pitted cherries
¼ cup sugar
1 ¼ cup red wine

1. In a sauté pan, place the cherries and sugar and heat together a bit to help the cherries give off some of there juices.
2. Add the red wine and continue simmering a few minutes to cook down slightly. Strain off the juice from the cherries and return it to the pan. Meanwhile start cooling the cherries. Continue cooking the juices to thicken slightly then add it back to the cherries and cool.

WHIPPED CREAM

½ cup heavy cream, chilled
½ tsp. sugar

1. Whip the cream with the sugar till stiff.
2. Keep chilled until ready to use.

ASSEMBLY

Kirsh, chilled

1. On a large plate, place one plug of chocolate sour cream cake.
2. Next to that, place a mini ramekin of the chocolate fudge pot.
3. Take a dessert spoonful of the cherry compote and make an arched swoosh of it across the plate.
4. Dip a dessert spoon in warm water and run it through the whipped cream to make a quenelle, then place that on the plate.
5. Finally pour a small shot of Kirsh into a tiny glass and place it next to everything.

Tower of Chocolate

Milk Chocolate Mousse

7 oz. milk chocolate
1 ½ tsp. powdered gelatin
¼ cup Kahlua
3 egg yolks
2 ½ Tbsp. sugar
4 Tbsp. white wine
2 cups heavy cream

1. Melt chocolate in a bowl over a pot of simmering water, being careful not to let chocolate get too hot.
2. Sprinkle gelatin on Kahlua, and set aside to soften.
3. Whisk together yolks, sugar and white wine in a bowl over boiling water until light and thick, approximately 10 minutes.
4. Melt gelatin and Kahlua over a pot of simmering water.
5. Whisk chocolate into yolk mixture, then gelatin.
6. In a separate bowl, whip cream to soft peaks and fold in.
7. Refrigerate for at least 2 hours.

Chocolate Spears

6" TALL AND 1" AT BASE IN A TRIANGULAR SHAPE

1 lb. bittersweet chocolate
1 cup sliced almonds, toasted

1. Temper chocolate.
2. Spread thinly on two 12 x 18-inch parchment lined pans.
3. Sprinkle with almonds.
4. Using a paring knife, cut into spears when it is set.

EXECUTIVE CHEF
Waldy Malouf

Chocolate Meringue

2 egg whites
½ cup superfine sugar, divided
1 tbs. cocoa

1. In a bowl of a standing mixer, whip egg whites until stiff.
2. Add ½ of sugar and whip until glossy, about 30 seconds.
3. Sift cocoa and remaining sugar together and fold into the egg whites.
4. Using a pastry bag fitted with a ½-inch plain tip, pipe out 2 ½-inch circles on parchment lined 12x18 pan and bake at 250° for 2 hours

Chocolate Cake (FOR TOP)

5 ½ Tbsp. unsalted butter, softened
¼ cup sugar
3 eggs, separated
½ cup almond flour
4 oz. semisweet chocolate, melted
½ tsp. vanilla

1. In a standing mixer fitted with the paddle attachment, beat the butter and sugar until light.
2. Add the yolks one at a time mixing well after each addition.
3. Add almond flour, chocolate and vanilla, mixing until combined.
4. In a clean bowl, whip whites to soft peak and fold into mixture.
5. Spread mixture into a 9 x 13 buttered, papered, and floured pan.
6. Bake at 350° for 15 minutes.

Brownie (FOR BOTTOM)

2 ½ oz. unsweetened chocolate
8 Tbsp. unsalted butter
1 cup sugar
2 eggs
1 tsp. vanilla
¾ cup flour
¾ cup chopped walnuts

1. Melt chocolate and butter together in a bowl over a pan of simmering water. Remove.
2. Whisk in the sugar, eggs and vanilla.
3. Fold in the flour and walnuts.
4. Pour into a 9 x 13 greased pan.
5. Bake at 350° for 15 minutes.

Assembly

1. Cut chocolate cake and brownie into 2 ½" circles with a plain round cutter.
2. Fill a pastry bag fitted with a ½" star tip with the milk chocolate mousse
3. Pipe a small quantity of milk chocolate mousse on plate and place brownie on the mousse.
4. Pipe a layer of milk chocolate mousse on brownie and top with the chocolate meringue.
5. Pipe another layer of milk chocolate mousse on the meringue and top with the chocolate cake.
6. Place 4 chocolate spears around the sides, using a little mousse as glue.

PRUNES AND CHESTNUTS CONFIT, ARMAGNAC ICE CREAM, AND CRUNCHY WALNUT TUILE

ARMAGNAC ICE CREAM
2 ¼ cups milk
¾ cup heavy cream
2 egg yolks
⅔ cup sugar
¼ cup milk powder
1 Tbsp. glucose
½ cup prunes
¼ cup Armagnac

1. Mix the milk, heavy cream, egg yolks, sugar, milk powder and the glucose in a saucepan and bring the mixture to a temperature of 185° in a bain-marie.
2. Soak the prunes in the Armagnac.
3. Add the soaked prunes to the warmed mixture and transfer it into an ice cream maker.
4. Freeze accordingly.

CHESTNUT CHANTILLY
1 cup heavy cream, whipped
¼ cup chestnut cream

1. Gently mix both ingredients together until stiff.

WALNUT TUILE
1 cup sugar
1 Tbsp. flour
2 tsp. walnut powder
4 Tbsp. milk
⅓ cup butter, melted
4 Tbsp. walnuts, chopped

1. Mix the sugar, flour and the walnut powder together.
2. Add the milk, butter, and walnuts until dough is slightly thickened.
3. Place a silpat sheet on a sheet pan or cookie sheet. Smear the mixture on the silpat sheet.
4. Bake in the middle of the preheated oven at 330° for 8 minutes, until golden.
5. Transfer a tuile with an offset spatula to a second sheet pan covered by a piece of nonstick aluminum foil Cut rectangles of 1 ½" x 5 ½".
6. You may need to reheat the tuiles for a few seconds frequently to prevent breakage and allow cutting.

PUFF PASTRY #1
2 cups butter, cold
1 cup flour

1. Mix the cold butter and the flour in a bowl until you receive a nice dough.
2. Reserve in the refrigerator for 3 hours.
3. On a floured surface, roll out the dough and form a square (½" thick). Reserve.

PUFF PASTRY #2
1 ¼ cups flour
½ Tbsp. salt
¾ cup butter, room temperature
¼ cup water
Icing sugar

1. Mix all of the ingredients quickly for about 2 minutes (do not knead!).
2. Reserve in the refrigerator for 3 hours.
3. On a floured surface, roll out the dough in a smaller square than the one done previously with pastry #1 (½" thick).
4. Put the square made with pastry #2 on top of the square made with pastry #1 and fold the bigger square like an envelope.
5. Roll out until ½" thick and fold it into 4.
6. Roll it again until ½" thick and fold it into 3.
7. Reserve for 2 hours. Then roll it again until ½" thick and fold it into 3.
8. Roll it as thin as possible.
9. Sprinkle some icing sugar onto both sides and bake at 350° until you see that the sugar caramelizes.
10. When cooled down, cut into rectangles 6" x 1 ½".

ASSEMBLY
1. Put one rectangle of the puff pastry on to a plate.
2. Place the ice cream on top and then the chestnut chantilly.
3. Garnish with a walnut tuile.

ALAIN DUCASSE
at the ESSEX HOUSE

PASTRY CHEF
Pierre Gatel

HONEY LEMON POLENTA CAKE

CAKE

1 lb. unsalted butter
5 cups sugar
4 cups all purpose flour
4 cups instant polenta
2 cups milk
2 cups cream
3 tsp. baking powder
1 tsp. salt
2 tsp. black pepper
1 Tbsp. vanilla
1 Tbsp. lemon oil
11 eggs
20 - 4 oz. disposable
aluminum molds

1. Combine cream and milk. Bring to a boil. Add polenta, stirring constantly for 15 minutes. Set aside.
2. In a mixing bowl, add the butter and sugar. Mix until smooth.
3. Mix in cooked polenta. Add eggs and mix until smooth.
4. Mix in dry ingredients and add lemon oil. Mix for 2 minutes.
5. Coat molds with a non-stick cooking spray. Fill each mold ⅔ high.
6. Bake at 350 degrees for 15 to 18 minutes.
7. Let cool and unmold. Garnish with Vin Santo sauce and whipped cream.

VIN SANTO SAUCE

4 cups honey
6 oz. Vin Santo
1 vanilla bean

1. Split the vanilla bean lengthwise and scrape the seeds.
2. Combine seeds and pod in a pot with Vin Santo & honey.
3. Bring mixture to a boil and lower to a simmer. Simmer for 3 to 5 minutes to cook out alcohol. Let cool.

GONZO

EXECUTIVE CHEF
Vinny Scotto

Chocolate Layer Cake

NEW YORK SWEETS

BLUE SMOKE

PASTRY CHEF
Jennifer Giblin

MAKES 1 10" CAKE
(3 LAYERS)

CHOCOLATE LAYER CAKE
3 ½ cups sugar
3 eggs
¾ cup canola oil
1 Tbsp. vanilla extract
1 ½ cups buttermilk
1 ½ cups cooled brewed coffee
2 ⅔ cups flour
1 ½ cups cocoa powder
1 ½ tsp. salt
1 ½ tsp. baking powder
1 Tbsp. baking soda

1. Butter and line three 10" round cake pans with parchment paper.
2. Preheat oven to 350º.
3. In the bowl of a mixer fitted with a whisk attachment, whisk together the sugar, eggs, and oil.
4. Add the vanilla, buttermilk, and coffee and continue to whisk.
5. Sift together the flour, cocoa powder, salt, baking powder, and baking soda.
6. Add all of the dry to the wet and whisk for 2 minutes on medium speed.
7. Scrape down the sides of the bowl and whisk for an additional minute to insure batter has no lumps.
8. Fill the cake pans half way and bake until cake springs back and the edges are coming away from the sides, about 20 minutes.

CHOCOLATE FROSTING
12 oz. bittersweet chocolate, chopped
10 oz. milk chocolate, chopped
¾ cup cocoa powder
⅓ cup brewed coffee
⅓ cup buttermilk
1 ¼ cups confectioners' sugar, sifted
4 sticks butter, softened
2 Tbsp. vanilla
⅛ tsp. salt
¼ cup corn syrup

1. Melt the chocolates together and let cool to room temperature.
2. In a saucepan, mix the cocoa powder, coffee, and buttermilk and cook over medium heat until boiling, make sure to continually stir with a spatula and scrape the bottom of the pan as not to let the cocoa scorch.
3. Let mixture cool to room temperature.
4. In a mixer, cream the butter, powdered sugar and the vanilla only until there are no lumps.
5. Add the cooled cocoa mixture and stir until incorporated.
6. Add the melted chocolate and fold in.
7. Finish with a pinch of salt and the corn syrup.

SLOW ROASTED PINEAPPLE WITH COCONUT SORBET AND GRANOLA CRUMBLE

SERVES 6 - 8

ROASTED PINEAPPLE

1 cup sugar

6 Tbsp. coconut milk

1 ½ bananas

Freshly squeezed juice of ½ lime

Pinch star anise

5 Tbsp. water

3 Tbsp. Malibu liquor

1 whole medium fresh ripe
pineapple, peeled, cut in half,
and cored

1. Preheat the oven to 150°.
2. Place sugar in a medium sized saucepan over medium heat and bring to a boil. Cook until it reaches a dark caramel.
3. Carefully add the remaining ingredients, except for the pineapples. Cook over low heat until the bananas are tender, Approximately 15 minutes.
4. Press through a fine-meshed sieve, making sure to push the bananas through completely.
5. Combine the caramel-banana purée and the fresh pineapples in a shallow, oven-proof baking dish and bake for 2 hours, basting and turning pineapple pieces every ten minutes. Remove and let cool.
6. Once cooled, cut each pineapple half in two pieces. Cut length wise into ¼ inch slices.
7. Refrigerate if making a day ahead.

GRANOLA CRUMBLE

2 Tbsp. dark brown sugar

⅓ cup plus 1 Tbsp. granola

2 Tbsp. butter, softened

2 Tbsp. all-purpose flour

¼ tsp. ground ginger

¼ tsp. ground cinnamon

¼ tsp. ground anise in powder

1. Combine all ingredients in a mixing bowl and set aside.
2. Refrigerate if making the day before.

COCONUT SORBET

15 oz. coconut purée

1 cup sugar

1 ½ cups water

Pinch lime juice

½ lime zest

1. In a large saucepan over medium heat, combine all the ingredients except for the lime juice and lime zest and cook until they reach 181° on a candy thermometer.
2. Mix well using a hand-held immersion blender.
3. Let the mixture develop overnight in the refrigerator.
4. Add the lime juice and zest before processing in an ice cream machine.

DANIEL

PASTRY CHEF
Jean Francois Bonnet

ASSEMBLY

1. Place the crumble mixture in an oven proof baking dish and heat at 300° until lightly warmed. Set aside.
2. Also warm the pineapple pieces just before serving. Sprinkle with the lime juice and set aside.
3. Divide the pineapple pieces between individual serving plates arranging them in a layered pattern.
4. Sprinkle pineapple with warmed crumble mixture.
5. Place scoops of sorbet alongside the pineapple and serve immediately.

NOTE FROM THE CHEF

This dessert is composed of three distinct elements each of which can be prepared one day ahead. However, the should be assembled just before serving. At DANIEL, we make the dessert with passion fruit sorbet on a merin base. For this recipe we have substituted coconut sorbet and eliminated the meringue. Not to worry, the crumb will add plenty of crunch.

MANGO CHEESECAKE

SERVES 9

MANGO CHEESECAKE FILLING
¾ lb. (12 oz.) cream cheese, cut into cubes and softened
¼ cup plus 2 Tbsp. sugar
3 eggs
1 ¾ cup (15 oz.) mango puree
2 tsp. lime juice

1. Preheat the oven to 300° Fahrenheit.
2. Place the cream cheese in a food processor and blend until smooth; add sugar and blend until smooth. Be sure to scrape down the sides with a spatula. Add eggs and pulse until well-blended. Pour the puree and the lime juice into this mixture and blend for 3 minutes.
3. Divide the mixture equally among the molds.
4. Take a deep baking pan and place the filled molds in the pan. Add cold water in the pan, so that the water level reaches ¾ the height of the molds.
5. Place the pan in the oven and bake for 45 minutes. Carefully turn the pan 180° and bake for another 20 minutes.
6. At this point, turn off the oven and leave the cheesecakes inside the oven for about 30 minutes. Remove molds from the pan and cool to room temperature. When the molds are cool, remove the foil and cover the bottom of each mold with plastic wrap. Chill overnight.

PASSION FRUIT-MANGO SAUCE
2 Tbsp. sugar
1 Tbsp. water
¾ tsp. corn syrup
2 Tbsp. unsalted butter
¼ cup passion fruit puree (available frozen food section of most markets)
¼ cup mango puree

1. Put sugar, water and corn syrup in a pan and caramelize over a low flame until golden brown, about 5 minutes.
2. Add butter immediately. After the butter melts halfway, add the puree and cook for another minute or so until smooth.
3. Cool the sauce and serve it at room temperature.

PASTRY CHEF
Surbhi Sahni

FOR THE CRUST
2 ½ cups all-purpose flour
⅔ cups confectioners' sugar
1 ½ sticks unsalted butter, cold
2 Tbsp. ice cold water
1 ½ cups slivered almonds
½ cup plus 2 Tbsp. clarified butter, melted

Note: The leftover crust can be stored in the refrigerator for up to two weeks. Prior to use, leave the crust out for about two hours, or microwave the quantity needed to soften the butter before use.

ASSEMBLY
Individual mango cheesecakes
½ cup sugar
Passion fruit-mango sauce
2 fresh mangoes, peeled and julienned (cut into very thin strips)

1. Preheat the oven to 350° Fahrenheit. Grease a 9" x 18" baking sheet and set aside.
2. Place the flour and sugar in a food processor and pulse to combine well. Add the butter and pulse until it has a bread crumb consistency; then add the water and pulse for 4 short bursts.
3. Flatten the mixture onto the greased baking sheet and cool in the refrigerator for 10 minutes. Bake for 10 minutes; then turn the baking sheet 180° and bake for an additional 10 minutes. Allow to cool on a rack.
4. Place the crust in a food processor and process into fine crumbs. Add the almonds and pulse in 4 short bursts. Add the ½ cup of clarified butter and pulse in 6 short bursts. The mixture should have a bread crumb consistency and should come together easily when handled.
5. Take the 9 individual cylinder molds (3" high and 2" in diameter; with no base) and cover one end with aluminum foil so that it completely covers the outside of the cylinder. Place on baking sheet foil side down.
6. Brush the inside of the mold with melted butter including the foil bottom. Put in a Tbsp. of the above prepared crust in each, press down to flatten it evenly at the bottom. Chill in refrigerator for 10 minutes.
7. Bake at 350° until the crust has a deep golden brown color, about 15 minutes. Remove from the oven and cool before adding the filling.

1. Take the cheesecakes and run a small knife around the edge of the mold to loosen them. Carefully push the cheesecake down so that the cheesecake stands on the crust base.
2. Sprinkle the top of each cake evenly with 1 ½ teaspoons of sugar and burn it with a propane or butane torch (available at gourmet supply stores). Circulate the torch for even coloring. Once the sugar melts, bubbles and turns to a golden color, allow to cool for about a minute before serving.
3. Place cheesecake in the middle of each plate; drizzle 2 tablespoons of sauce around it and put some julienned mango in a heap on the side.
4. Serve immediately.

NOTE FROM THE CHEF
These small cheesecakes should be made one day before serving. This recipe makes 9 individual servings and as it is a fragile cheesecake, I would not recommend converting it into one large cake. Clarified butter can be found in the ethnic food section of markets or at healthfood stores – also known as Ghee.

Calamansi Gelatin

1 qt. yellow watermelon puree

1 ½ cups Calamansi honey

¾ cup unflavored gelatin powder

Assorted fruits, chopped (mango, kiwi, pineapple)

1. Mix 3 cups of the puree with the honey.
2. Place remaining cup of puree in a bowl and sprinkle gelatin on the surface.
   Allow gelatin to soften, approximately 5 minutes.
3. Place bowl of gelatin over a pan of simmering water to melt gelatin.
4. Add gelatin to puree mixture.
5. Place in molds and refrigerate to set.
6. Decorate plates with chopped fruit and place gelatin on top.

EXECUTIVE CHEF
Roberto Pagan

CHOCOLATE HEAVEN

CHOCOLATE CAKE
2 Tbsp. all purpose flour
2 Tbsp. extra bitter cocoa powder
2 egg whites
2 eggs
⅓ cup plus 2 Tbsp. granulated sugar
3 egg whites
3 Tbsp. superfine sugar

1. Preheat the oven to 350°.
2. Sift together the flour and cocoa powder.
3. Beat the 2 egg whites, eggs, and granulated sugar until fluffy and double in volume.
4. Whisk the 3 egg whites with the superfine sugar until stiff peaks form.
5. Fold the egg mixture into the egg white mixture. Gently foldin the flour mixture.
6. Bake for 10 to 12 minutes.

CRÈME ANGLAISE
1 ¼ cups milk
¼ cup granulated sugar
6 egg yolks
2 sheets gelatin, bloomed

1. Mix together the milk and ½ the sugar. Bring to a boil.
2. Whisk together the other ½ of the sugar with the egg yolks.
3. Pour the hot milk into the egg yolks in a steady stream while whisking constantly.
4. Put in a double boiler and cook until thick while stirring constantly with a wooden spoon.
5. Soak sheets of gelatin in cold water until they become soft. Remove softened sheets from water and squeeze out the excess.
6. Add in the bloomed gelatin and strain.

WHITE CHOCOLATE MOUSSE
4 oz. white chocolate, chopped
1 oz. cocoa butter
½ cup hot crème anglaise
1 cup whipped cream

1. Melt the white chocolate and cocoa butter.
2. Add in the hot crème anglaise and stir until smooth.
3. Let cool.
4. Whip cream to soft peaks. Fold into crème anglaise/chocolate mixture.

EXECUTIVE CHEF
Nicholas Lee

Milk Chocolate Mousse

½ cup hot crème anglaise
5 ½ oz. milk chocolate, chopped
¾ cup whipped cream

1. Melt the milk chocolate and add in the hot crème anglaise. Stir until smooth and let cool.
2. Whip the cream until soft peaks and fold in to cool crème anglaise/chocolate mixture.

Dark Chocolate Mousse

½ cup plus 2 Tbsp. hot crème anglaise
4 oz. extra bitter dark chocolate
¾ cup plus 2 Tbsp. whipped cream

1. Melt the dark chocolate and add in the hot crème anglaise. Stir until smooth and let cool.
2. Whip the cream until soft peaks and fold in to cool crème anglaise/chocolate mixture.

Assembly

1. In pyramid-shaped molds, put a layer of white chocolate mousse, then a layer of milk chocolate mousse, and then a layer of dark chocolate mouse.
2. Top with a slice of chocolate cake.
3. Refrigerate for at least 2 hours before serving.
4. Decorate with creme anglaise.

CASABLANCA CAKE

HAZELNUT SUCCESS BISCUIT

⅓ cup confectioners' sugar
⅓ cup roasted hazelnut flour
⅔ cup granulated sugar
2 large egg whites

1. Sift confectioners' sugar and then combine it with the hazelnut flour.
2. In a bowl of a standing mixer, start whipping the egg whites on medium speed. When the whites become foamy and opaque, gradually add granulated sugar until egg whites reach stiff peaks.
3. Using a rubber spatula, gently fold the flour/confectioners' sugar mixture into the egg white mixture.
4. Using a pastry bag fitted with a ½ inch plain tip, pipe two different size spiral discs on a sheet tray lined with parchment. One disc should measure 5-inches in diameter and the second disc should measure 3-inches in diameter. Bake in preheated convection oven at 325º for 40 minutes.
5. After it is done baking, store in a cool, dry place.

ORANGE "CREMEUX"

½ cup half and half
½ cup white chocolate (chopped into pieces)
Zest of one orange

1. In saucepan, combine half and half and orange zest and bring to a boil.
2. Add chopped white chocolate and stir until ingredients are well blended.
3. Cover with plastic wrap and refrigerate for about 2 hours until it reaches a creamy consistency.

GLACAGE REGAL

6 cups Jivara (milk) chocolate (available in specialty stores or use regular milk chocolate)
⅓ cup Amande, granulated almonds (or regular chopped blanched almonds)
½ cup Huile, soy oil (or corn oil)

1. Melt the Jivara (milk) chocolate.
2. Stir in granulated almonds and soy oil, set aside.

CARAMELIZED ALMONDS

⅜ cup granulated sugar
⅛ cup water
1 cup whole, blanched almonds

1. In a saucepan, cook water and sugar to 257º and then add the almonds while keeping the flame low.
2. Constantly stir the almonds with a wooden spoon until it reaches light caramel color.
1. Pour the almond mixture on top of a parchment paper lined tray.
2. Measure ⅓ cup of caramelized almonds and chop them into small pieces.

ITALIAN MERINGUE

¾ cup granulated sugar
2 Tbsp. water
2 egg whites
1 pinch sea salt

1. In a standing mixer fitted with the whisk attachment, whip egg whites on low speed.
2. While the whites are whipping begin cooking sugar and water in sauce pan up to 250º.
3. Increase the speed of the mixer to medium, and carefully pour cooked sugar syrup into whipped egg whites and continue whipping until the bowl cools down and the whites are stiff and increased in volume.

PRALINE CREAM

½ cup hazelnut praline paste
6 tbsp. butter, softened
Italian meringue, already prepared
⅓ cup caramelized almonds, already prepared

1. In a bowl, whisk praline paste and very soft butter together (note: this mixture should not be in the form of a liquid but very soft)
2. Using a rubber spatula, gently fold in the Italian meringue and then the chopped, caramelized almonds.

ASSEMBLY

1. In a 5 ½" half sphere mold, buttered and lined with plastic wrap, scoop about 7 spoonfuls (4 oz.) of praline cream and spread on the interior surface of the dome.
2. Insert the 3" hazelnut biscuit upside down.
3. Pipe in the praline cream up to the mid-level.
4. Using a pastry bag fitted with a ½" plain tip, pipe a 3" diameter disc of orange Cremeux on top of the praline cream.
5. Pipe in the praline cream almost to the top, leaving ½" away from the surface of the dome.
6. Place 5" hazelnut biscuit on top to level up to the surface of the dome.
7. Finish the cake by making the surface of the cake neat with the rest of the praline cream and freeze.
8. When it's frozen, dip the mold in hot water and place your fingers on the edge of the cake and slide them out of the mold.
9. Place the cake on the cardboard and by using a ladle; glaze the entire dome with a glacage regal twice.

FAUCHON
PARIS

EXECUTIVE CHEF
Florian Bellanger

Romeo & Juliet

2 cups catupury cheese at room
temperature (or regular cream cheese)
1 cup guava paste
1 tsp. vanilla extract
2 cups heavy cream
1 cup white chocolate, melted
1 can guava (halves in syrup)
Mint leaves

1. In the bowl of a standing mixer, whisk the cream cheese, guava paste, and vanilla until very pale and soft.
2. In a clean bowl, whip the cream until soft peaks form.
3. Drizzle the chocolate into the cream cheese mixture and fold together with the whipped cream.
4. Using a pastry bag fitted with a ½" plain tip, use this cream to fill the walls and bottom of 4 round dessert molds, about 3" each. Refrigerate for 2 hours.
5. Unmold and garnish the side with thin slices of guava and 2 mints leaves on top.

EXECUTIVE CHEF
Samira Soares

FIREBIRD APPLE TRIO

CALVADOS SOAKED BABA, PECAN STUFFED LADY APPLE AND FENNEL-APPLE SALAD

SERVES 8

BABA

½ oz. fresh yeast
⅓ cup milk, warm to 100º
1 ½ Tbsp. granulated sugar
3 eggs
1 ⅓ cup bread flour
1 ½ Tbsp. butter, unsalted
1 golden delicious apple, peeled
1 tsp. kosher salt
8 Tbsp. Mascarpone confectioners' sugar
non-stick cooking spray

1. Crumble the yeast onto warm milk. Stir to dissolve.
2. Add sugar and stir until incorporated.
3. Whisk in all the eggs.
4. Stir the wet mixture into the flour until a smooth, wet dough is formed.
5. Cut butter into ½" squares and place them on the top of the dough to further soften.
6. Cover the dough with plastic wrap to proof until the dough has doubled in size.
7. Shred apples on coarse grater and fold into the dough with the salt.
8. Spray the baba molds lightly with the non-stick cooking spray.
9. Fill the molds ¼ full with the dough.
10. Cover with plastic wrap and allow to rise again until the baba molds are ¾ full.
11. Bake at 350º until golden brown crust forms on top.
12. Remove from molds.
13. When room temperature, soak the baba in warm soaking syrup (see recipe).
14. Garnish each with 1 tablespoon of Mascarpone and dust with confectioners' sugar.

SOAKING SYRUP

4 cups water
2 cups sugar
½ cup Calvados

1. Boil water and sugar for 1 minute.
2. Remove from heat and add Calvados.
3. Reserve warm.

CANDIED NUTSP

1 cup water
1 cup sugar
2 cups whole pecans

1. Boil water and sugar for 2 minutes.
2. Remove from heat.
3. Add pecans and stir until all surfaces are coated.
4. Strain off excess liquid and place the nuts on a non-stick cookie sheet.
5. Bake at 325º for 7 minutes.
6. Remove and cool.
7. When cool, coarsely chop.

LADY APPLES

1 stick butter, melted
8 lady apples, peeled in a striped pattern and cored out from the underside
½ cup sugar
Candied Nuts

1. Brush the outside of the apples with melted butter. Roll in sugar.
2. Fill the cavity of each apple with the chopped candied nuts.
3. Carefully invert the apple onto a small roasting pan, making sure that the nuts do not fall out.
4. Bake at 350º for 20 minutes, or until tender.
5. Remove from oven and serve warm.

FENNEL – APPLE SALAD

1 head fresh fennel
2 golden delicious apples, peeled
3 Tbsp. grape seed oil
1 Tbsp. cider vinegar
Pinch kosher salt

1. Slice the fennel and apples into a fine julienne.
2. Toss the vegetable and fruit mixture with oil, vinegar and salt.
3. Reserve.
Note – This process should not be done in advance.

FireBird

PASTRY CHEF
Jacqueline Zion

Hazelnut Dacquoise

Serves 10

Sponge
3 egg whites
¼ cup powdered sugar
¾ cup plus almond flour
1 ⅓ cups hazelnuts, ground

1. Whip egg whites into soft peaks with half of the sugar.
2. Then stir in the other half of the sugar with the almond flour and hazelnuts
3. Fold the whites and flour mixture together with a spoon
4. Spread sponge batter about ¼" thick on two parchment paper lined baking sheets
5. Bake at 400° for 5 to 7 minutes until light golden color.
6. Remove from oven and let cool.
7. Invert and peel the paper off the sponge. Let cake cool further.

Filling
1 ¼ lbs. (20 oz.) dark semi-sweet chocolate
6 Tbsp. butter
½ cup sugar
10 eggs, separated, room temperature
2 cups heavy cream
1 ½ tsp. dark rum
¾ tsp. vanilla

1. Melt chocolate and butter together in double boiler. Remove from heat and cool slightly.
2. Beat half of the sugar with the egg yolks until the mixture is light and creamy and double in volume.
3. Beat egg whites to soft peaks. Gradually add remaining sugar and beat until stiff peaks form.
4. Whip cream to stiff peaks.
5. Fold chocolate/butter mixture into yolks, and then fold in whipped cream, rum and vanilla. Chill to set.

EXECUTIVE CHEF
Marshall J.P. Orton

Assembly
1. Cut sponge into fingers 2 ½" by ¾".
2. Spread with the chocolate mousse.
3. Cover with fine sheet of chocolate.
4. Spread with the chocolate mousse.
5. Cover with fine sheet of chocolate for garnish.

Banana Chocolate Chip Cake with Peanut Butter Frosting

Serves 10 to 12

Cake

2 sticks plus 3 Tbsp. butter

2 cups sugar

1 Tbsp. vanilla

3 eggs

3 very ripe, large bananas, mashed with a fork

3 cups plus 3 Tbsp. flour

1 ½ tsp. baking powder

1 ½ tsp. baking soda

1 tsp. salt

1 cup buttermilk

1 cup semi sweet chocolate chips

1. Butter and flour 3 – 9" pans using the 3 tablespoons of butter and the 3 tablespoons of flour.
2. In an electric mixer, cream the butter and sugar together until light, fluffy, and pale yellow.
3. Add the vanilla and eggs, one at a time, blending in after each one is added.
4. Blend the mashed bananas into the batter.
5. Mix the flour with the baking soda, baking powder, and salt.
6. Alternating, add the flour mixture and the buttermilk in batches, beginning and ending with the flour. Mix just to blend. Do not over mix.
7. Stir in the chocolate chips.
8. Divide the batter between the 3 cake pans and bake at 350° for 30 minutes. If a toothpick is inserted in the center and comes out clean, the cakes are done.
9. Let the cakes cool to room temperature before frosting.

Frosting

1 lb. (2 - 8 oz. pkgs.) cream cheese, softened

1 cup (2 sticks) butter, softened

1 cup creamy peanut butter

4 cups powdered sugar, sifted

1 Tbsp. vanilla

1 Tbsp. light corn syrup

1. With an electric mixer, cream the cream cheese and butter together until fluffy and white in color.
2. Add the peanut butter and blend.
3. Add the powdered sugar, vanilla, and corn syrup and blend until smooth.
4. Refrigerate for 30 minutes before you frost the cakes.

PASTRY CHEF
Michele Weber

CHOCOLATE LAVA CAKE

MAKES 5 INDIVIDUAL CAKES

12 oz. semi-sweet chocolate
2 Tbsp. butter
8 oz. egg yolks
8 oz. sugar
12 oz. egg whites
½ cup cake flour
1 tsp. salt

1. On a double boiler, melt chocolate and butter.
2. In a separate bowl, add egg yolks and 4 ounces of the sugar.
3. When chocolate is melted, whisk slowly into the yolks until well combined.
4. Combine the flour and salt and incorporate it into the chocolate mixture.
5. In an electric mixer, whip remaining sugar and egg whites to stiff peaks.
6. Slowly fold whipped egg whites into chocolate mixture.
7. When well incorporated, bake in molds at 350º for 9-11 minutes

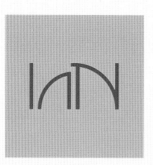

EXECUTIVE CHEF
Ian Russo

STRAWBERRY SHORTCAKE WITH CREAM BISCUITS AND CRÈME FRAICHE

SERVES 8

STRAWBERRY FILLING
2 pints strawberries, quartered
1½ cups sugar
½ vanilla bean
1 strip of lemon rind (1" x 1")

1. Add strawberries, sugar, and lemon rind to a saucepan.
2. With a knife, carefully split vanilla bean lengthwise and scrape out seeds. Add both seeds and pod to saucepan.
3. Cook on medium heat for 20 minutes.
4. Let cool.

CREAM BISCUITS
2 cups all purpose flour
2½ tsp. baking powder
½ tsp. salt
1 Tbsp. sugar
1½ cups heavy cream

1. In a large mixing bowl, using a fork or whisk, lightly combine the flour, baking powder, salt, and sugar.
2. With a wooden spoon (or stand mixer fitted with the paddle attachment), mix in the heavy cream until just combined. Do not over mix.
3. Lightly dust a rolling pin and surface with flour, and roll the dough to a thickness of about 1¼".
4. Cut in rounds to make 8 biscuits, with a lightly dusted, round cutter or glass.
5. Bake on a cookie sheet, lined with parchment, at 350° for 15 minutes, or until golden brown.
6. Let cool.

ASSEMBLY
1 cup crème fraiche, whipped

1. Cut the biscuits in half.
2. Spoon some of the strawberry mixture on top.
3. Place a dollop of crème fraiche on the side and serve.

LANDMARC

CHEF
Frank Proto

CAFÉ ET BEIGNET

SERVES 4

DOUGHNUTS

1 medium size Idaho potato
2 cups all purpose flour
½ cup sugar
¼ tsp. baking soda
1 ¼ tsp. baking powder
½ tsp. salt
½ tsp. cinnamon
½ tsp. nutmeg
2 Tbsp. melted butter
½ cup sour cream
1 egg
1 qt. canola oil
½ cup sugar mixed with 1 Tbsp.
cinnamon for dusting

1. Peel, dice, and boil the potato until tender.
2. While the potato is still warm, put it through a ricer and reserve ½ cup.
3. Sift the dry ingredients into a bowl of a standing mixer fitted with a paddle attachment.
4. Combine the wet ingredients and then add them to the dry ingredients.
5. Mix for one minute at low speed and then add the ½ cup of potato.
6. Mix on medium speed for ten minutes.
7. Wrap in plastic wrap and chill the dough for three hours.
8. Heat 4 inches of canola oil in a heavy bottomed pan over medium heat, until oil reaches 375º F.
9. On a lightly floured surface, roll the chilled dough to a thickness of ¼" and cut into 1" squares.
10. Fry 5 or 6 pieces of dough at a time for approximately 1 minute, until golden brown. Make sure to turn doughnuts often for even color.
11. Toss the warm doughnuts in the cinnamon sugar and serve.

COFFEE SYRUP

½ cup water
½ cup sugar
3 Tbsp. instant espresso powder

1. In a sauce pan bring the water and sugar to a boil and cook over medium heat until the sugar fully dissolves. Add the espresso powder.
2. Pass the syrup through a fine mesh strainer and cool on an ice bath.
3. Portion the syrup between four glasses.

MILK SHAKE

1 pint coffee ice cream
½ cup milk
1 cup heavy cream, whipped

1. In a blender, mix the coffee ice cream and milk to desired thickness.
2. Pour into the four glasses over the coffee syrup.
3. Garnish with whipped cream and serve with warm doughnuts.

Marseille

PASTRY CHEF
Nick Morgenstern

Gaufrette au Chocolat

Gaufrette
2 cups flour
4 cups milk
8 eggs
1 tsp. butter
Fleur de sel (sea salt)
Pinch of sugar

1. Place the flour into a bowl. Form a well in the middle and add the eggs, fleur de sel, and the sugar.
2. With a whisk, slowly incorporate the eggs into the flour and then add the milk slowly. Mix well until there are no lumps.
3. Add the melted butter to the mix.
4. Reserve the mix in the refrigerator for ½ a day. Resting the mix is important in determining the quality of the gaufrette.
5. When ready to use the mix, check consistency. It should be like a pancake batter, not thin or liquid. If it is too thin, correct as needed by adding more flour.
6. Cook in pizzelle maker for 2 to 3 minutes.

Chocolate Caramel
1½ cups sugar
1¼ cups light corn syrup
3 Tbsp. butter, room temp.
3 Tbsp. fleur de sel
½ cup (4 oz) bittersweet chocolate, chopped
1¼ cups heavy cream
3 sheets of gelatin

1. In a heavy-bottomed 4 to 5 quart pot over medium-high heat, combine the sugar and the corn syrup. Continue stirring until a mahogany color is reached evenly throughout (340°). Add the butter in cubes and stir vigorously until dissolved. Lower heat to low.
2. At the same time in another pot, bring the heavy cream to a boil and melt the chocolate over a double boiler or in a bowl sitting over a pot of gently simmering water, not touching the water.
3. Take the sugar mixture off the heat and add the melted chocolate and heavy cream. Stir continuously until the caramel is dissolved.
4. Return to heat and cook the mixture until it reaches 230° to 240° and remove from heat.
5. Pour into a sheet pan lined with parchment paper and cool.

Chocolate Mint Chantilly
3.5 oz. bittersweet chocolate
2 tsp. sugar
1⅓ cups heavy cream
Peppermint powder, to taste

1. Combine chocolate and sugar in a bowl.
2. Bring cream to a boil and pour over chocolate and sugar. Refrigerate.
3. Whip in a bowl resting on another bowl of ice, slowly.
4. When the chantilly has reached a soft, velvety consistency, sprinkle some mint powder and fold. Make sure not to over-whip.

Fleur de Sel

EXECUTIVE CHEF
Cyril Renaud

Assembly

6 oz. 73.5% chocolate for glazing, melted

2 gaufrette, cut into circles

Cocoa nibs, toasted (available in gourmet stores or online)

Chocolate mint powder

Fleur de sel

1. With a brush, glaze one of the gaufrettes with melted chocolate and sprinkle the toasted cocoa nibs on top, sparingly. Set aside in the refrigerator.
2. With the circle cutter you used to cut the gaufrettes, cut a disk of the chocolate caramel. Then take a smaller disc and cut a circle from the middle of the chocolate caramel turning it into a donut-like ring.
3. Place the donut ring of chocolate caramel on top of one of the gaufrettes.
4. Fill the middle with some of the chocolate mint chantilly.
5. Sprinkle a bit of mint powder on top of the chantilly and a bit of fleur de sel on top of the chocolate caramel.
6. Place the other gaufrette on top and press down with a plate until it looks like a cookie.
7. Sprinkle a little fleur de sel on top of the gaufrette and place a couple of leaves of baby chocolate mint on top.
8. Finish with a quenelle of chocolate sorbet or ice cream.

LAVENDER HONEY GLACE

PISTACHIO CRUNCH
1 lb. white chocolate
3 Tbsp. pistachio paste
14 oz. Paliette Feulitine

1. In a bowl over a pot of simmering water, melt white chocolate with pistachio paste.
2. Once completely melted, fold in Paliette Feulitine.
3. Spread evenly on a parchment lined half sheet pan.
4. Refrigerate and cut into 3" x 1" rectangles.

PISTACHIO SUGAR
¾ cup roasted pistachios
¼ cup sugar

1. Combine nuts and sugar in a food processor.
2. Process until the consistency of sand.

MACERATED CHERRIES AND CHERRY PLUM WINE SYRUP
2 cups pitted cherries
2 Tbsp. sugar
2 Tbsp. Cherry Brandy
½ cup plus 2 Tbsp. Plum Wine

1. Place all ingredients in a saucepan, over medium heat until liquid boils.
2. Remove cherries from pan and reserve them. Continue to boil the liquid for 10 minutes, until reduced and thickened. Set aside to cool.

LAVENDER HONEY GLACE
2 sheets gelatin
¾ cup honey
½ cup lavender syrup (recipe below)
4 egg whites
2 cups heavy cream, whipped
2 cups chopped roasted pistachios
⅓ cup chopped candied lavender

1. Place gelatin in a bowl of ice cold water to soften, set aside.
2. In a saucepan, heat honey and lavender syrup over medium heat until mixture boils.
3. In the bowl of a standing mixer fitted with the whisk attachment, whip egg whites until frothy. Slowly pour in hot syrup. Continue to whisk until mixture cools.
4. Squeeze the excess water out the gelatin and melt it over a low heat in the syrup pot.
5. Pour gelatin into egg whites and whip until stiff peaks form.
6. Remove bowl from mixer and fold whipped cream into egg whites.
7. Fold nuts and lavender into mixture.
8. Spread into a mold and freeze.
9. Cut into 3" x 1" rectangles.

LAVENDER SYRUP
¼ cup sugar
¼ cup water
2 Tbsp. fresh lavender

1. Combine all ingredients in a saucepan.
2. Cook over medium heat until sugar dissolves.
3. Let lavender steep for 10 minutes and pour through a fine mesh strainer.

APRICOT FRUIT LEATHER
2 cups apricot puree
¼ cup sugar

1. Combine ingredients and spread thinly on a silpat.
2. Bake at 225° for 30 minutes.
3. Cut 1" x 4" strips and form into waves.

NOBU
NEW YORK CITY

PASTRY CHEF
Jessica Isaacs

ASSEMBLY
1. Place Pistachio Crunch on a plate.
2. Place Lavender Honey Glace on Pistachio Crunch.
3. Place three cherries on top of glace.
4. Put a piece of Fruit Leather on top of cherries.
5. Take a pastry brush and dip into Cherry Plum Wine Syrup.
6. Brush syrup on plate.
7. Sprinkle pistachio sugar in a thin line.

COCONUT AND PASSION FRUIT PARFAIT WITH WILD BERRY SAUCE

PASSION FRUIT CREAM

3 egg yolks
2 eggs
½ cup sugar
6 Tbsp. passion fruit purée
(Goya brand is available in
the Latino frozen section)
5 oz. butter, softened

1. In a stainless steel mixing bowl, whisk together the yolks, whole eggs, sugar, passion fruit purée, and cook over simmering water, while whisking, until frothy and light like a zabaione.
2. Cool.
3. Slowly add the soft butter.
4. Refrigerate for 24 hours.

COCONUT MOUSSE

½ oz. granulated gelatin
½ cup water
1 ¾ cups whipping cream
1 ½ cups coconut puree
⅓ cup coconut paste

1. Sprinkle gelatin over ½ cup water in small bowl and allow to bloom.
2. Whip cream to stiff peaks.
3. Mix together the coconut puree and the coconut paste.
4. Fold in the whipped cream and the gelatin.

COCONUT BISQUIT

¼ cup plus 2 Tbsp. almond flour
2 Tbsp. high gluten (bread) flour
¼ cup plus 2 Tbsp. coconut powder
1 ¾ cups sugar
6 egg whites

1. In a bowl, sift together the almond flour, high gluten flour, coconut powder, and ½ the sugar.
2. With a mixer, whip the egg whites to soft peaks. Gradually add the remaining sugar and whip to medium peaks.
3. Carefully fold the egg whites into the flour mixture, being careful not to deflate.
4. Spread onto on a parchment lined baking sheet and cook at 340° for 5 minutes

WILD BERRY SAUCE

½ cup sugar
1 Tbsp. water
2 cups wild berries
½ cup water

1. Put the sugar in a saucepan.
2. Add the tablespoon of water and stir gently over medium-high heat with a wooden spoon until the sugar is dissolved.
3. Allow to boil until it reaches the light caramel stage (338°).
4. Add wild berries and ½ cup of water.
5. Bring to a boil.
6. Cool down and pass the berry mixture through a sieve.

ASSEMBLY

1. Cut the bisquit into rectangles.
2. Place a bisquit on a plate.
3. Put a scoop of passion fruit cream and a scoop of coconut mousse, side by side on the bisquit.
4. Put another bisquit on top.
5. Add another layer of passion fruit cream and coconut mousse.
6. Top with a third bisquit.
7. Refrigerate the cake for at least five hours.
8. Serve the dessert with the wild berry sauce and fresh berries.

Casa Tua
MIAMI

EXECUTIVE CHEF
Oscar Bonelli

RIZ AU LAIT TART

RIZ AU LAIT
5 cups milk
1 ¼ cups sugar
12 cinnamon sticks
15 cardamom pods
2 nutmeg, smashed
10 pcs. of whole pepper
2 cups Arborio rice
1 cup milk
½ cup sugar
4 egg yolks
8 oz. cream,
whipped soft

1. In one pot, combine the 5 cups of milk, the 1 ¼ cups of sugar, and spices and warm on the back burner, stirring every so often.
2. In another pot, place rice and enough water to cover by 3". Bring water to a boil and then drop to a simmer, stirring regularly. Cook rice halfway (it will have more than just a bite). When it reaches this stage, strain and rinse some of the starch off under cool water.
3. Then place rice in pot with milk/spice mixture and continue simmering until fully cooked. The rice should have some body to it. It shouldn't be mushy but it also shouldn't be crunchy in the middle.
4. Place in a pan with plastic wrap touching surface to cool.
5. When ready to use, measure out 5 cups of the rice mixture.
6. Bring the 1 cup of milk and ¼ cup of the second sugar to a boil.
7. Whisk together yolks and remaining ¼ cup of sugar.
8. Pour boiling liquid into yolks in a steady stream while whisking constantly.
9. Return liquid to pot and return to heat and cook while stirring gently with a wooden spoon, until nappe is achieved (a line is formed without blurring edges when finger is run down back of spoon).
10. Add into the rice mixture.
11. Fold in the whipped cream last.

PASTRY CHEF
Daniel Skurnick

ORANGE PEKOE SORBET
2 qt. water
¼ cup trimoline
½ cup plus 1 Tbsp. dextrose
¼ cup plus 1 Tbsp. sugar
15 orange pekoe tea bags

1. Combine water, trimoline, dextrose and tea.
2. Warm to steaming and then add the sugar. Bring to a boil.
3. Allow to steep overnight.
4. Strain and spin in ice cream machine.

KUMQUAT COMFITURE
½ lb. (1 cup) kumquats
1 qt. simple syrup

1. Slice kumquats in half. Scoop out flesh and discard. Place shells in pot and cover with water. Bring to a boil and strain. Repeat 2 more times.
2. Cover with simple syrup and simmer until done.

PISTACHIO TUILE
¾ cup pistachio nuts
¾ cup sugar
½ tsp. corn syrup
1 stick plus 1 Tbsp. butter

1. Toast pistachios and grind coarsely when cool.
2. Combine sugar and corn syrup. Warm, then add butter. Cook to 227°.
3. Add nuts and mix well.
4. Pour between 2 silpats or two pieces of parchment paper and roll with a rolling pin very, very thin.
5. Bake at 350° for 8 minutes. While hot, cut into strips.

PHYLLO SHELL
Phyllo dough, store bought
2 Tbsp. clarified butter (available in health stores or ethnic sections of markets)
Pinch of confectioners' sugar

1. Butter parchment paper.
2. Place one sheet of phyllo dough on top. Butter and cover with another.
3. Repeat until you have used 5 sheets.
4. Put butter and confectioners' sugar on the top sheet.
5. Cut to large size ring molds.
6. Bake with pie weights at 325° for 5 to 6 minutes.

VANILLA ORANGE SAUCE
2 ¼ cups water
2 ½ cups sugar
6 Tbsp. corn syrup
2 vanilla beans
1 nutmeg, smashed
2 cinnamon sticks
Zest of 7 oranges

1. Blanch the orange zest, by submerging in boiling water for 30 seconds. Strain.
2. In a pot, combine all other ingredients and simmer until tacky.
3. Strain and then add the orange zest.

CANDIED PISTACHIOS
½ cup pistachio nuts, very coarsely ground
1 Tbsp. simple syrup
1 tsp. sugar in the raw

1. Coat nuts with syrup until just wet. Then put on the sugar.
2. Bake at 350° until golden.

ASSEMBLY
1. In a phyllo shell, place a thin layer of kumquats.
2. Put the rice pudding on the kumquats and then top it off with a few more kumquats.
3. On the other side of the plate, place some candied pistachios.
4. Place a scoop of the sorbet on top of the nuts.
5. Use the vanilla orange sauce to decorate the plate.

LEMON VERBENA NAPOLEON CRÈME BRULE

SERVES 10

NAPOLEON LAYERS
1 pound phyllo dough
(or 24 sheets)
2 sticks butter, melted

1. Place one sheet of phyllo dough on counter top.
2. Brush lightly with melted butter and place another sheet of phyllo dough on top.
3. Continue stacking the phyllo with butter until there are 8 sheets of phyllo dough with brushed butter between each sheet.
4. Cut out ten 3" circles with a round cutter.
5. Repeat steps 1 through 4, two more times until all the phyllo dough is finished.
6. On 2 half-sheet pans lined with parchment paper, place 15 circles on each pan. Top with another piece of paper, and then another sheet pan to weigh it down.
7. Bake at 350º for about 20 minutes, until golden brown.
8. Cool completely.

CRÈME BRULE CREAM
1 qt. heavy cream
1 packed cup of fresh lemon verbena
½ cup sugar, divided
8 egg yolks
½ cup crushed amoretti cookies

1. In a saucepan, over medium heat, cook heavy cream, lemon verbena, and half the sugar until simmering.
2. Strain the verbena, puree it, and then strain back into the cream.
3. Add the remaining half the sugar to the yolks. While whisking the yolks, pour in some of the hot cream. Pour the yolk mixture back into the hot cream, stirring constantly.
4. Strain into a bowl and sprinkle with the crushed cookies. Place into a water bath and bake in a preheated oven, 350º for 40 minutes.
5. Cool completely.

RASPBERRY SAUCE
1 qt. fresh raspberries
1 cup sugar
3 Tbsp. lemon juice

1. Puree the berries with ½ cup of sugar and the lemon juice.
2. Taste and add more of the sugar by the spoonful if needed.
3. Sieve to remove seeds and seed residue.
4. Refrigerate in a covered bowl. Sauce will keep for a day or two.

GRAND CENTRAL OYSTER BAR & RESTAURANT

PASTRY CHEF
Janos Noka

ASSEMBLY
2 pints fresh raspberries
Granulated sugar

1. On one piece of phyllo, put 1 tablespoon of cream on the center of the disc.
2. Place fresh raspberries around the outside edge. Cover with another disc of phyllo.
3. Repeat as in step one with cream and raspberries.
4. Cover with a third and final disc on top.
5. Sprinkle with granulated sugar and caramelize with a hand held torch.
6. Serve with raspberry sauce.

TROPICAL STICKY CARROT CAKE

SERVES 4

½ cup dates, pitted
⅓ (heaping) cup carrots, shredded
1 ⅛ cup coconut milk
½ vanilla bean, split and scraped
½ stick butter
¾ cup vanilla sugar
2 eggs
¾ cup all purpose flour
2 tsp. baking soda
1 tsp. baking powder
¼ tsp. cinnamon
Pinch of nutmeg

1. Preheat oven to 325°. Spray 6 – 3" ramekins (¾ cup capacity) with non-stick cooking spray.
2. Place dates in the bowl of a food processor and pulse until they are finely chopped.
3. Combine the chopped dates, shredded carrots, coconut milk, and vanilla bean in a saucepot. Bring the mixture to a boil, remove from heat. Set aside.
4. In an electric mixer, fitted with a paddle attachment, cream the butter and vanilla sugar until it is light and fluffy. Add the eggs, one at a time, scraping the bowl after each addition.
5. In a small bowl, combine the flour, baking soda, baking powder, and spices.
6. Using a rubber spatula, fold the flour mixture into the butter mixture. Then gently fold in the date mixture (remove vanilla bean pod).
7. Divide batter evenly among the 6 prepared ramekins and place on a baking sheet.
8. Bake for 20 to 30 minutes, or until it springs back when lightly touched.
9. Allow to cool for 10 minutes in the ramekins. Serve warm.

LAS OLAS

PASTRY CHEF
Sarah Magoon

ICE BOX TOWER

SERVES 12

CHOCOLATE COOKIE
1 ¼ cup all purpose flour
¼ tsp. salt
1 ½ sticks of butter, softened
¾ cup confectioners' sugar
1 egg
1 tsp. vanilla
¾ cup high quality cocoa powder

1. Sift the flour and salt together, set aside.
2. In a standing mixer fitted with the paddle attachment, cream the butter & sugar until light.
3. Add the egg and vanilla, mixing until combined.
4. Mix in cocoa powder until incorporated.
5. Add salt and flour in 3 additions. Do not over mix.
6. Form into 2 disks, wrap and chill for 2 hours.
7. Roll dough on flat surface until about ³/₁₆" thick.
8. Cut as many cookies as possible with a 2 ½" round cookie cutter.
9. Bake at 325° for 7-9 minutes.

CHOCOLATE PASTRY CREAM
2 cups half and half
6 egg yolks
½ cup sugar
3 Tbsp. flour
¼ tsp. salt
2 tsp. vanilla
4 oz. bittersweet chocolate, melted & cooled

1. Heat half and half until just beginning to simmer.
2. In separate bowl, whisk yolks, sugar, flour and salt until pale yellow and fluffy.
3. Gradually pour 1 cup of hot half and half in the egg yolk mixture.
4. Whisk SLOWLY.
5. Pour egg mixture back into pot with remaining half and half.
6. Cook over medium heat, stirring constantly for 5-8 minutes, until slightly thick.
7. Strain. Add vanilla and cooled chocolate.
8. Cover with plastic wrap; set over ice bath and cool to room temperature.
9. Refrigerate overnight.

Note — Do not overcook. Do not let pastry cream get too thick. It will firm up in refrigerator overnight. It does not spread nicely if too thick.

SWEETENED WHIPPED CREAM
2 cups heavy cream
2 tsp. vanilla
2 tsp. confectioners' sugar

1. Place cream, vanilla and confectioners' sugar in a chilled metal bowl.
2. Whip until soft peaks form.

Matt Lewis
Renato Poliafito

ASSEMBLY
1. Place a cookie flat side down and spread thinly with chocolate pastry cream.
2. Place another cookie on top and spread with sweetened whipped cream.
3. Repeat steps one and two until dessert is seven cookies tall.

WHITE CHOCOLATE RASPBERRY CHEESECAKE

SERVES 8-12

1 cup graham cracker crumbs
¼ cup melted butter
1½ lbs. cream cheese
½ cup sugar
1 cup heavy cream
1 tsp. vanilla extract
3 oz. white chocolate, melted
3 eggs
1 pint raspberries, fresh or frozen

1. Preheat the oven to 275°.
2. Melt butter and drizzle into the graham cracker crumbs to make moist enough to hold together but not overly oily.
3. Place the crumb mixture into a 10" spring mold and press down to make the crust ¾" in thickness.
4. Melt the white chocolate by cutting into small pieces and either placing in a bowl over a pan of hot water (off the heat) while stirring, or in the microwave for no more than 5 seconds at a time, stirring after each. (Do not overheat or the chocolate will seize up and become unusable)
5. In a mixer or with a blender, combine the cream cheese and sugar and whip until smooth. (Remember to scrape down the sides at least 3 times)
6. Add the heavy cream and vanilla. Continue to whip mixture.
7. Add one egg at a time, blending each until incorporated before adding the next egg.
8. When thoroughly incorporated, add the white chocolate and blend lightly until just combined.
9. Pour into the spring mold, over the crust.
10. Place half of the raspberries in the mixture and place in the oven on a baking sheet.
11. Place a pot with water in the oven with the cheesecake and cook for about 1 hour, until almost set.
12. Let cool and set in the refrigerator for at least 3 hours before serving.

ASSEMBLY
One cup heaving whipping cream
2 Tbsp. sugar
1 tsp. vanilla

1. Whip cream until mounds begin to form.
2. Add sugar and vanilla; continue whipping just until stiff peaks form.
3. Place a wedge of cheesecake on a plate.
4. Top with raspberries and whipped cream.

SHAFFER
OYSTER BAR & GRILL
CITY

EXECUTIVE CHEF
Jay Shaffer

CHEF DE CUISINE
Kary Goolsby

Ghujia

SERVES 4

PASTRY
1 cup (2 sticks) butter
1 cup semolina
1 tsp. salt
½ cup raisins
¼ cup pistachios
¼ cup coconut flakes
¼ cup cashew nuts
Syrup (recipe below)
Puff pastry, store bought

1. Preheat oven to 325°. Line baking sheets with parchment or waxed paper.
2. In a small saucepan, melt the butter. Stir in semolina and cook for 10 minutes, until golden brown.
3. Add the salt, raisins, pistachios, coconut flakes, and cashew nuts. Continue to cook for another 5 minutes, while tossing.
4. Add the syrup and keep on low heat until separated from the saucepan.
5. Refrigerate 1 to 2 hours, until cold.
6. Cut the puff pastry into 4" circles.
7. Drop teaspoons of filling in the pastry.
8. Brush the edges with water or egg and fold over, sealing edges together.
9. Place on parchment lined pans and bake for 10 minutes, until puffy and golden.

SYRUP
3 cups water
2 cups sugar
Cardamom seeds for flavor

1. Bring water, sugar and cardamon seeds to a boil.
2. Continue to cook, while stirring, until the sugar dissolves.
3. Cool.

PASTRY CHEF
Claudio Quito

TEMPURA CHOCOLATE CHEESECAKE WITH PASSION FRUIT AND SHISO

PASSION FRUIT SAUCE

1 cup pure passion fruit puree/pulp (available at specialty stores)

¾ cup granulated sugar

2 passion fruit, bottom & top shaved slightly so they can stand on either end & cut in half

1. Put ½ cup of passion fruit puree and sugar into a heavy bottom stainless steel 2 qt. pot over medium heat. Stir to dissolve.
2. Small bubbles will begin to form and get larger. As the caramel begins to turn a light amber color, the caramel will be foamy. Do not stir (or sugar lumps will form), only swirl pan to check color. Another minute or two and caramel should be a medium brown amber color.
3. Immediately remove from heat and carefully pour in ¼ cup of the reserved passion fruit puree and swirl pan to incorporate. Add the remaining ¼ cup of puree. Scoop out the fresh passion fruit into the sauce. Stir and chill.

SHISO

8 shiso leaves (available in specialty stores)

1 cup semi sweet chocolate chips, melted and cooled

1. Brush chocolate over 4 shiso leaves on a small holed rack or on parchment paper, then transfer to a clean plate or parchment and refrigerate until ready to use.

CHEESECAKE

SHOULD BE MADE 12 HOURS IN ADVANCE

1 cup semisweet chocolate chips

12 oz. cream cheese, softened

½ cup sugar

2 eggs

¼ cup sour cream

1 tsp. vanilla extract

¼ cup Wondra flour

2 eggs, beaten

2 cups panko bread crumbs, lightly crushed by hand

3 cups canola oil

1. Melt chocolate chips in a double boiler or in a bowl fit over a pot of barely simmering water (do not let the bowl touch the water), stirring occassionally, until melted. Cool for 15 minutes.
2. Combine cream cheese and sugar in a large bowl or mixer (paddle attachment preferred). Beat on medium speed, scraping bowl occasionally, until creamy, approximately 2 minutes. Add the eggs, one at a time, beating well after each addition. Reduce speed to low, add melted chocolate, sour cream and vanilla. Beat until well mixed.
3. Pour cheesecake into a parchment lined 9"x 9" baking dish, cover with aluminum foil poked with holes so that the top does not brown or form a crust. Bake at 350º for 1 hour or until just set ¾ of the way. Remove foil, cool, and refrigerate over night.
4. Set up an assembly line for Wondra flour, beaten eggs and panko bread crumbs.
5. Using a ¾ oz. scoop, scrape cheesecake into level scoops and drop onto the Wondra flour.
6. When all balls are scooped (5 or 6 per person) roll them around in the flour to evenly coat, then pick them up one at a time and form them so they are perfectly round.
7. Roll them in the egg mixture, let the excess egg drip off, and then completely cover them in the panko crumbs.
8. Keep refrigerated until ready to use, then chill in the freezer for 15 minutes to firm (don't freeze).
9. Deep fry in batches in a pot deep enough so that oil comes up at least 2" at 350º until golden brown. Remove from oil with a slotted spoon and drain on a paper towel. Serve warm.

The Mansion Inn

EXECUTIVE CHEF
Pamela Nicholas

ASSEMBLY

1. Place one chocolate shiso leaf off-center on plate with an un-coated leaf next to it, overlapping slightly.
2. Stack warm tempura cheesecake in the middle of the plate. Fill the passion fruit cups with the sauce and place next to the cheesecake.
3. Use extra passion fruit sauce and melted chocolate to decorate plate.
4. Serve with chopsticks.

MILK CHOCOLATE CHIP BAKED ALASKA

MILK CHOCOLATE MALT ICE CREAM

2 cups cream
2 cups milk
¼ cup malt powder
2 cups sugar, divided
7 egg yolks
1 cup milk chocolate, finely chopped
¼ cup bittersweet chocolate, chopped into ¼" inch pieces

1. In a saucepan, boil the cream, milk, malt powder, and 1 cup of sugar.
2. Whisk the yolks with the remaining sugar. While whisking, pour some of the hot cream mixture into the yolks. Return yolk mixture into remaining cream and cook, stirring constantly over low heat until mixture thickens and coats the back of a spoon, approximately one minute.
3. Add chopped milk chocolate to hot ice cream mix and let stand for 1 minute. Whisk smooth.
4. Cool over ice.
5. Spin in ice cream machine and fold in chopped bittersweet chocolate pieces.
6. Scoop ice cream into round molds 3" in diameter and place graham cracker rounds (recipe follows) on top.
7. Allow to freeze overnight.

GRAHAM CRACKER

12 oz. crisco
1 lb. light brown sugar
8 oz. all purpose flour
1 lb. whole wheat flour
½ tsp. salt
1 ¼ cups buttermilk

1. In a mixing bowl with a paddle attachment, mix together the crisco and brown sugar until fluffy.
2. In a separate bowl, mix the flours and salt.
3. Slowly add the flour to the crisco mixture until incorporated.
4. Add in the buttermilk.
5. Roll crust into sheets and freeze.
6. Cut out 3" circles and bake at 325° until golden brown.

MERINGUE

3 egg whites
⅔ cup sugar

1. In the bowl of a standing mixer, whisk whites and sugar together while heating over a pot of simmering water.
2. When hot and foamy, and sugar is dissolved, place on mixer and whip until cooled and it forms stiff peaks.

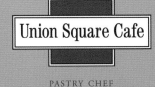

PASTRY CHEF
Emily Isaac

ASSEMBLY

1. Invert the molded ice cream onto a plate, graham cracker side face down.
2. Spread the meringue over the ice cream.
3. Using a hand held propane torch, brown the meringue

CARNIVAL DE MANZANA

CARAMEL
½ cup sugar
A few drops of lemon juice
1 Tbsp. water
1 oz. hot water

APPLE FLAN
1 cup heavy cream
½ cup evaporated milk
½ cup condensed milk
3 Tbsp. light brown sugar
4 eggs
3 egg yolks
3 Tbsp. sugar
1 cup green apple puree
2 ½ oz. Calvados

1. Combine the sugar and lemon juice in a non-reactive saucepot with one tablespoon of water.
2. Cook on medium heat until sugar is golden brown.
3. Take caramel off the fire and add 1 ounce of hot water. Swirl the mixture until uniform.
4. Divide evenly into 22 – 2 oz. aluminum containers (the caramel should just cover the bottom of the container).
5. Allow to cool and set.

1. In a non-reactive saucepot, combine heavy cream, evaporated milk, condensed milk, and light brown sugar.
2. Scald milk mixture.
3. Whisk eggs and sugar in a medium sized bowl.
4. Add ½ of the hot milk mixture into eggs and sugar whisking constantly.
5. Add egg mixture into milk, whisking constantly.
6. Add puree and strain.
7. Add calvados and mix well.
8. Pour into caramel lined cups.
9. Bake at 300° for 15 to 20 minutes in a hot water bath covered with aluminum foil.

SUSHISAMBA

PASTRY CHEF
Vera Tong

ROSE PETAL JELLO

ORANGE WHIPPED CREAM

1 cup heavy cream
½ tsp. orange oil
1 Tbsp. powdered sugar

1. Allow whisk and metal bowl to stand in freezer for about 15 minutes.
2. Whip all ingredients together until semi-stiff peaks form.

JELLO

¼ cup cold water
¼ cup cranberry juice
2 Tbsp. unflavored, granulated gelatin
4 ½ cups boiling water
¼ cup sugar
2 Tbsp. grenadine
1 ½ Tbsp. rose water
1 tsp. orange flower water
Organic rose petals

1. In a large bowl, sprinkle gelatin over the cold water and cranberry juice. Let stand about 2 minutes, until gelatin is softened.
2. Dissolve sugar in boiling water, then pour over gelatin and stir until incorporated.
3. Gently stir in grenadine, rose water, and flower water.
4. Pour into clear serving glasses.
5. When partially set, carefully push a rose petal into the center of the jello in each glass.
6. When completely set, top with whipped cream.

EXECUTIVE CHEF
Carrie Starcher

EAT AND DRINK
MANGIA E BEVI

1 ½ tsp. lemon zest
½ cup Gran Gala or other orange liqueur
⅓ cup orange juice
½ cup white wine
3 cups peaches, diced
1 ½ cups fresh apricots, diced
1 ½ cups grapes
1 cup plums, diced
2 cups cantaloupe, diced
1 cup strawberries, quartered
1 cup blueberries
1 cup blackberries
1 cup raspberries
3 cups watermelon, seeded and diced

1. Place the lemon zest, Gran Gala, orange juice, and wine in a large saucepan. Heat over medium heat until it starts to simmer and then cook for 5 minutes. Remove from heat and cool for 10 minutes.
2. Mix the fruit together in a large bowl. Pour the marinade over and mix well. Cover the bowl with plastic wrap and refrigerate for 2 hours, or up to 24 hours.

CHERRY COMPOTE
½ cup sugar
½ cup water
4 cups bing cherries or sour cherries

1. In a large saucepan, mix together sugar, water, and cherries. Bring to a low boil and cook for 15 to 20 minutes, until the cherries start to soften.
2. Remove from flame and let cool.
3. Any leftover compote can be stored in the refrigerator for a few days.

TO SERVE
1 Tbsp. mint leaves, chopped
½ cup sugar
1 pt. vanilla ice cream, softened (or sorbet of your choice)
1 cup heavy cream
½ cup cherry compote

1. You need 8 large glasses.
2. Spoon layers into each glass as follows: 4 tablespoons of fruit, 4 tablespoons of ice cream, 2 tablespoons of fruit, 2 tablespoons of heavy cream, 1 tablespoon of fruit, and 1 tablespoon of cherry compote.
3. Top with a flag or umbrella and serve.

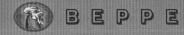 BEPPE

EXECUTIVE CHEF
Chris Deluna

*This recipe is from Cesare Casella's forthcoming cookbook
"True Tuscan", published by Harper Collins.

CARAMELIZED PINEAPPLE

PINEAPPLE

1 cup wild flower honey

2 Tbsp. butter

1 pineapple, peeled, cored and cut in half lengthwise

Pink peppercorns, to garnish

Licorice powder, to garnish

Thai chili, to garnish

Maldon sea salt, to garnish

Anise hyssop, to garnish

1. Preheat the oven to 400°.
2. Heat the honey and butter in a large sauté pan over medium heat.
3. Add the pineapple and baste the pineapple until well coated.
4. Transfer pineapple and honey to a small roasting pan and place in the oven. Baste the pineapple every 5 to 8 minutes until the pineapple is caramelized and cooked through.
5. Remove the pineapple from the honey mixture and chill.
6. Cut the pineapple into bite size pieces.
7. Garnish the pineapple with pink peppercorns, licorice powder, thai chili, sea salt, and anise hyssop.

SUGAR TUILE

1 cup fondant

½ cup glucose

½ cup isomalt

1. Combine all the ingredients and bring to soft crack stage on a candy thermometer.
2. Pour the mixture onto parchment paper and roll into a thin sheet.
3. Cut the sugar into 2" squares and reserve.

SPICED GELEE

1 cup water

½ cup sugar

1 tsp. allspice

1 tsp. cinnamon

¼ tsp. clove

2 gelatin sheets, softened in ice cold water

1. In a sauce pan over medium heat, bring the water, sugar and all of the spices to a boil. Remove from heat and steep for 10 minutes.
2. Add softened gelatin and pour through a fine mesh strainer.
3. Chill gelee in square molds until firm. Reserve.

ASSEMBLY

Vanilla beans

1. Take a new straight vanilla bean and skewer the spice gelee cube.
2. Next, skewer the garnished pineapple.
3. Cover the pineapple and gelee with the sugar tuile.
4. Warm slightly with a hand held propane torch, enough to melt sugar over the pineapple.
5. Serve immediately.

ALINEA

EXECUTIVE CHEF

Grant Achatz

CHICAGO

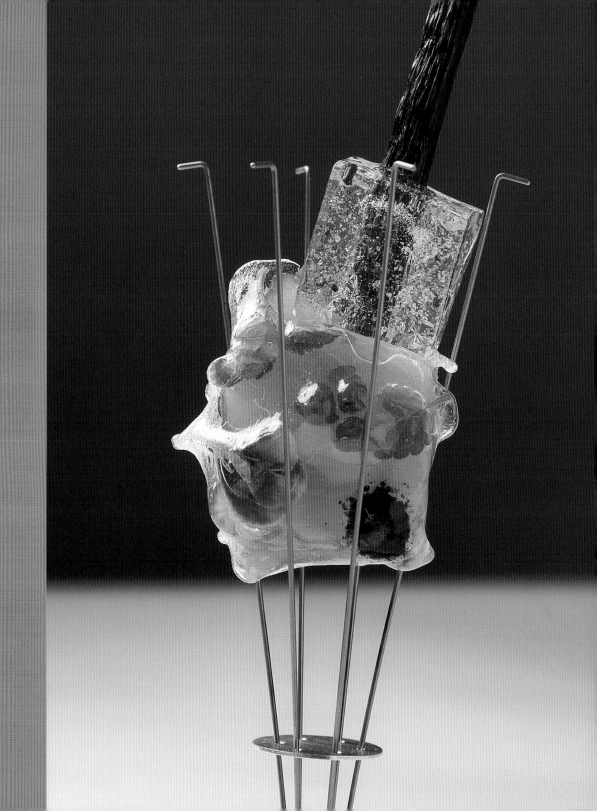

SPUMA DI RICOTTA

RICOTTA CHEESE MOUSSE WITH BLOOD ORANGE SALAD

SERVES 4

3 cups ricotta cheese
¼ cup superfine sugar
2 cups heavy cream
1 blood orange, peeled and segmented
1 pint fresh strawberries, cleaned and cut into quarters
1 sprig fresh mint

1. In a glass bowl, gently mix the orange, strawberries, and fresh mint. Refrigerate for 1 hour.

2. In a mixer, slowly cream the ricotta cheese and sugar. Blend until smooth.

3. In a separate bowl, with a mixer, whip the heavy cream until itforms soft peaks.

4. Carefully fold the whipped cream into the ricotta cheese mixture until it is fully incorporated.

TO SERVE

1. Spoon the salad mixture into a serving bowl or glass.

2. Dollop the ricotta mousse on top.

NAPLES 45

RISTORANTE E PIZZERIA

EXECUTIVE CHEF
Chris Deluna

RASPBERRY CHAMBORD PANNA COTTA

SERVES 6-8

1 cup milk, divided
1 Tbsp. powder gelatin
2 ½ cups heavy cream
¼ cup sugar
½ cup Chambord Liqueur
½ cup raspberry jam
½ pint fresh raspberries
Fresh mint

1. Take ½ cup of milk and sprinkle the gelatin on the surface.
2. Bring the remaining milk, 1 cup of cream, and sugar to a boil.
3. Add the gelatin mixture into the hot milk and whisk until melted.
4. Place milk/cream mixture over an ice bath and whisk gently until cool, but not cold.
5. Add the Chambord.
6. In a mixing bowl, whip the remaining 1 ½ cups of cream until it begins to hold its shape. Fold in to mixture.
7. Place a spoonful of raspberry jam in the bottom of a glass and then pour the Panna Cotta mixture on top of it.
8. Carefully place the glass in the refrigerator for at least three hours, until set.
9. Serve cold after decorating with berries and/or fresh mint.

THE FOUR SEASONS
RESTAURANT
PASTRY CHEF
Patrick Lemble

French Toast, Brown Butter Ice Cream, and Raisin Puree

RAISIN PUREE
4 cups raisins
1 Tbsp. cinnamon
2 cups water

1. Boil raisins with water until almost dry.
2. Puree in blender until smooth.
3. Add cinnamon.

RAISIN PAPER
4 cups raisins
1 egg white

1. Soak raisins in cold water overnight.
2. Puree in blender with a small amount of water.
3. Add egg white and blend well.
4. Spread mixture in a thin layer on a sheet pan and dry in the oven at 200° for 2 hours.
5. Break into pieces.

MAPLE GELLE
3 Tbsp. maple syrup
1 cup cold water
1 tsp. gellan

1. Hydrate the gellan in cold water.
2. Boil the maple syrup.
3. Blend together and chill.

FRENCH TOAST
1 loaf brioche bread
4 cups milk
¼ cup rum
1 cup confectioners' sugar
2 tsp. cinnamon
¼ tsp. nutmeg
4 whole eggs, whipped
Clarified butter for cooking

1. Cut bread into 2" x 1" x 2" oblongs.
2. In a bowl, mix the milk, rum, confectioners' sugar, cinnamon, nutmeg, and eggs.
3. Soak the brioche in the rum milk mixture for 20 minutes.
4. Pan fry the brioche cubes in clarified butter until golden.

BROWN BUTTER ICE CREAM
4 cups brown butter milk (recipe below)
⅓ cup plus 1 Tbsp. milk powder
½ cup sugar
4 tsp. trimoline (available in specialty stores)
⅔ cup glucose
1 ¼ cups cream
3 whole eggs

1. Place brown milk and milk powder in a pan and bring to a simmer.
2. Add sugar, trimoline, and glucose. Bring to a boil.
3. Add the above mixture in a steady, slow stream into the whole eggs while whisking constantly.
4. Add cream and chill.
5. Run in an ice cream machine according to manufacturer's instructions.

BROWN BUTTER MILK
2 lbs. butter
1 qt. milk

1. Brown butter in pan until dark.
2. Carefully whisk in milk, being aware that mixture may splatter.
3. Set in refrigerator overnight.
4. Pierce the butter, which will have solidified, and strain milk.

BACON BITS
Bacon slices

1. Fry a little bacon in a pan and chop into small pieces.

wd~50

PASTRY CHEF
Sam Mason

Arctic Circle with Blueberry Sorbet, Passion Fruit Curd and a Honey Tuille

Blueberry sauce

¾ cup blueberry puree
1 ½ Tbsp. sugar
¼ vanilla bean
½ tsp. agar-agar powder (available in health food stores)

1. Bring blueberry puree, sugar and vanilla bean to a boil.
2. Add the agar-agar and cook for about 5 minutes, until dissolved, stirring the whole time.
3. Strain and cool.

Blueberry sorbet

1 cup blueberry puree
¾ cup plain yogurt
½ cup 10x (powdered) sugar
3 Tbsp. heavy cream
1 ½ Tbsp. honey
½ vanilla bean

1. Mix blueberry puree, yogurt and sugar.
2. Bring heavy cream, honey and vanilla bean to a boil and then strain over the blueberry mix.
3. Cool.
4. Turn in an ice cream machine.

Passion fruit curd

½ cup passion fruit puree
1 lemongrass, sliced thin
⅔ cup sugar
5 egg yolks
14 Tbsp. butter, cut into 1" dice

1. Bring passion fruit puree to a boil together with the lemongrass.
2. Mix the egg yolks with the sugar and then pour over the passion fruit puree.
3. Put over a double boiler and cook, stirring constantly, until the mixture thickens.
4. Strain and then whisk in the butter.

Arctic Circle

¾ cup sugar
¼ cup water
3 egg whites
¾ cup plus 2 Tbsp. crème fraiche
¼ cup goat cheese
3 gelatin sheets, soaked in cold water for 15 minutes, with excess squeezed out
1 cup heavy cream
½ cup sour cream

1. Cook the sugar and water to a hard boil.
2. Whisk the egg whites on medium speed in a mixer for 2 minutes and then add the sugar and water slowly with the whisk going on low speed.
3. When the water and sugar are incorporated in the egg whites, raise the speed to medium and keep whisking until completely cool. Set meringue aside in the freezer.
4. Put 1/2 the crème fraiche, all of the goat cheese and soaked gelatin sheet in a pot.
5. Over medium heat, melt until dissolved. Set aside to cool.
6. Whip the heavy cream until soft peaks and put in refrigerator.
7. Combine the gelatin crème fraiche mix with the remainder of the crème fraiche and sour cream. Mix until smooth.
8. Add the meringue and mix until smooth. Then add the whipped heavy cream and mix until fully incorporated.
9. Pipe into cylinders 3'-1 ½" and freeze.
10. When completely frozen use an apple corer to cut a hole in the middle.

Honey tuille

5 Tbsp. butter, softened
¼ cup honey
½ cup 10x (powdered) sugar
⅓ cup plus 1 Tbsp. flour
3 egg whites

1. Whisk the butter and the honey until smooth.
2. Sift in the sugar and flour slowly and then whisk in the egg whites slowly.
3. Using 2 tablespoons of the mix at a time, spread it out in any shape you wish and on a silpat or parchment paper lined sheet pan.
4. Bake at 400 degrees until golden brown, 6-8 minutes.
5. Remove quickly and bend over rolling pin.

Assembly

1. Fill the hole in the arctic circle with the passion fruit puree.
2. Put the tuille and a quenelle of the sorbet on top.
3. Put the sauce on the side.

AQUAVIT

CHEF/OWNER
Marcus Samuelson

EXECUTIVE CHEF
Nils Noren

Pralin Au Gout D'Enfance

Peanut Crunch with White Chocolate Cake

Serves 10

Crunch

1 oz. white chocolate

⅓ cup peanut butter

⅓ cup praline paste

2 ½ oz. feuilletine

(available at specialty stores)

1. Melt white chocolate in a bowl over a pot of simmering water. Do not let it get too hot.
2. In a separate bowl, combine the peanut butter and praline paste and place it over the pot of simmering water, to warm the mixture.
3. Place these 3 ingredients into the bowl of a standing mixer, fitted with a paddle attachment.
4. Add the feuilletine and mix well.
5. Set this mixture aside in a warm place.

White Chocolate Mousse

2 cups heavy cream

8 oz. white chocolate

3 egg yolks

3 egg whites

1. In the bowl of a standing mixer, whip the cream until firm. Refrigerate until ready to use.
2. Melt the white chocolate in a bowl over a pot of simmering water. Set aside in a warm place.
3. Whisk the egg yolks in a medium bowl.
4. In the bowl of a standing mixer, whip the whites to stiff peak.
5. Using a rubber spatula, fold the whites into the yolks.
6. Fold in the melted white chocolate.
7. Fold in the whipped cream. (It is important to fold in the cream without stopping until mixed in order to obtain a smooth consistency. If you stop folding or fold incompletely, the chocolate will harden and you will have little pieces of un-melted chocolate throughout the mousse).
8. Refrigerate the mousse until ready to use.

PASTRY CHEF
Laurent Richard

DACQUOISE

¼ cup almond flour
¼ cup confectioners' sugar
1 egg white
1 Tbsp. sugar

1. Sift the almond flour and confectioners' sugar together onto a piece of parchment paper.
2. In the bowl of an electric mixer on medium speed, whip the egg whites until they double in volume.
3. Gradually add the sugar and whip until stiff, approximately 2 minutes.
4. Using a rubber spatula, fold the dry ingredients into the whites.
5. Fill a pastry bag fitted with a ¼" plain tip. Pipe the mixture onto a parchment lined 12 x18-inch sheet pan in an 8-inch square.
6. Bake at 400° on a double tray for approximately 15 minutes or until the dacquoise is lightly browned.
7. Set aside to cool.

ASSEMBLY

10 oz. milk chocolate, melted for spraying

1. Place an 8-inch square frame on a parchment lined cookie sheet.
2. Place the baked dacquoise into the bottom of the frame.
3. Spread the warm crunch mixture over the dacquoise until flat.
4. Fill the frame with the mousse and smooth the surface.
5. Freeze overnight, un-mold and cut in 2" squares.
6. Using a paint gun, spray with melted chocolate.

BLUEBERRY COOLIS

BLUEBERRY ICE CREAM

1 cup heavy cream
½ cup milk
¼ cup corn syrup
¼ cup plus 2 Tbsp. sugar
3 egg yolks
1 cup blueberry puree

1. Bring heavy cream and milk to a boil over medium heat.
2. Add corn syrup and sugar and whisk until dissolved.
3. Whisk milk and cream mixture into egg yolks slowly, as not to curdle the yolks.
4. Pass mixture through a fine sieve and whisk in blueberry puree.
5. Chill in an ice bath. When cool, run through ice cream maker following machine's directions

VANILLA TUILE BUTTER

6 Tbsp. butter
3 Tbsp. honey
½ vanilla bean
¼ cup plus 2 Tbsp. all purpose flour
¾ cup 10x sugar
2 egg whites

1. Cream together butter, honey, and vanilla bean until light and fluffy, approximately 6 to 8 minutes, scraping down the sides at least 2 times.
2. Sift together the sugar and flour and add them to the butter honey mixture.
3. Begin mixing slowly and add egg whites. Mix until smooth and creamy.
4. Spread in desired shape and bake at 300° for 6 to 10 minutes, until golden brown.

VANILLA ICE CREAM

1 cup heavy cream
½ cup milk
½ vanilla bean
¼ cup sugar
2 Tbsp. corn syrup
3 egg yolks

1. In a medium saucepot, combine heavy cream, milk, and vanilla bean with pod over medium heat and steep for about 5 minutes.
2. Whisk in sugar and corn syrup and mix until dissolved.
3. Slowly whisk hot liquid into egg yolks, so as not to curdle the yolks.
4. Strain through a fine sieve and chill in an ice bath.
5. When cold, run through ice cream maker following machine's directions.

AUREOLE

EXECUTIVE CHEF
John Miele

BLUEBERRY COOLIS

2 cups blueberry puree
½ cup sugar
⅓ cup corn syrup
½ cup water
Juice from ½ of a lemon

1. Combine all ingredients in a medium saucepot.
2. Cook on medium heat and simmer about 6 to 10 minutes, stirring occasionally until slightly thick or it coats a spoon.
3. Strain through a sieve and cool in an ice bath. Serve chilled.

OATMEAL STREUSEL

5 oz. light brown sugar
¼ cup sugar
½ cup plus 2 Tbsp. oats
⅓ cup plus 1 Tbsp. cake flour
1 ½ tsp. cinnamon
¼ tsp. salt
1 stick butter
¾ tsp. vanilla extract

1. Chop butter into small cubes and allow to soften at room temperature.
2. Combine all dry ingredients until uniform.
3. Work butter into dry ingredients slowly, by hand.
4. Transfer mixture to a food processor and mix until crumbly.
5. Remove and work in vanilla until just combined.

FRUIT

1 Tbsp. Riesling
Juice from ½ of a lemon
1 ½ Tbsp. cornstarch
¼ cup sugar
¼ tsp. cinnamon
Pinch of salt
2 nectarines - cut into medium dice
1 pt. fresh blueberries
½ tsp. rosemary, chopped

1. Combine Riesling and lemon juice in a small mixing bowl.
2. Whisk in dry ingredients slowly, do not form lumps.
3. Stir in rosemary.
4. Toss fruit gently in liquid.
5. Take the pie crust and fill it with the fruit. Top it with the oatmeal streusel and bake at 300° for 20 to 25 minutes.

PIE CRUST

1 stick plus 1 Tbsp. butter
1 cup plus 2 Tbsp. all purpose flour
½ cup plus 1 Tbsp. 10x sugar
1 egg

1. Chop butter into small cubes and refrigerate.
2. Sift together flour and sugar in a mixing bowl.
3. Add butter to dry ingredients and mix on low speed until butter is broken down and has a mealy texture.
4. Add egg and mix until dough comes together.
5. Refrigerate for about 1 hour.
6. Roll to about ⅛" thick and line a muffin tin with the dough.
7. Cover with paper and fill the paper with beans to weigh down dough.
8. Bake with beans at 300° for approximately 10 to 12 minutes.
9. Remove beans and continue to bake approximately 6 to 8 minutes more, until golden brown.

ASSEMBLY

1. Make a small pool of blueberry coolis and surround with a fine brunoise nectarine (finely diced).
2. Place baked cobbler in the middle of the coolis.
3. Top with ice cream and place the vanilla tuile on top of the ice cream.
4. You may also use a puffed pastry stick as a garnish.

BANANA PASTRY CREAM

BANANA PASTRY CREAM

1 qt. milk

1 cup sugar

1 cup plus 3 Tbsp. cornstarch

8 egg yolks

1 stick butter

3 large ripe bananas

1 tsp. salt

1 tsp. vanilla extract

1 Tbsp. banana extract or banana liquor

1. Bring milk to a boil in a large pot.
2. Whisk together the sugar, corn starch, and egg yolks until smooth and lightly whipped.
3. Dice the butter and set aside.
4. Puree bananas (the mushier and bruised the better) and measure one cup of puree.
5. Ladle a bit of the boiling milk into the egg yolk mix and whisk until smooth. Then pour all of the egg mixture slowly back into the boiling milk pot and whisk vigorously until it begins to thicken and bubble in the center.
6. Remove from heat and whisk in the butter, banana puree, salt, vanilla extract and banana liquor.
7. Pour into a bowl and cover with plastic wrap.
8. Refrigerate until cool.

BLUE FIN

PASTRY CHEF
Rob Valencia

CAKE LAYER

2 ½ sticks butter

1 ½ cups granulated sugar

3 large eggs

3 cups all purpose flour

2 tsp. baking soda

1 tsp. baking powder

1 tsp. salt

¼ cup sour cream

3 large ripe bananas

1 cup toasted walnuts, crushed

1. Cream butter and sugar in electric mixer until light and fluffy.
2. Add the eggs one at a time.
3. Sift together dry ingredients.
4. Dice up the bananas and add to the sour cream.
5. Add the dry ingredients alternating with the sour cream/banana mix. Then continue to mix for one minute while adding in the walnuts.
7. Spread the batter on to a 9" x 9" baking pan and bake at 325° for 12 minutes. Cool completely. Cut 2" disks.

CARAMEL SAUCE

4 cups sugar

Water

2 cups heavy cream

1. Place the sugar in a heavy-bottomed saucepan.
2. Add enough water to just cover the sugar.
3. Bring to a boil and continuously stir until the mixture reaches a dark caramel color.
4. Remove from heat.
5. Slowly add in the heavy cream while whisking.
6. Bring back to a boil.
7. Strain and chill.

ASSEMBLY

8 ounces melted white chocolate

1 roll of 2-inch acetate, cut into 9 ½ - inch strips

12 - 3-inch ring molds

Banana Pastry Cream

Banana Cake layer

2 large bananas

½ cup light brown sugar

1. Spread melted white chocolate on each acetate strip. Wrap around the inside of a 3" ring mold with chocolate facing inward. Chill to set.
2. Place the cake disk in the bottom of the ring mold. Beat the pastry cream by hand until smooth and pour into the ring mold, filling up to the top.
3. Chill the mold for 1 hour to set pastry cream.
4. Prepare thin slices of banana, cut on a diagonal and caramelize with brown sugar using a hand held propane torch. Place standing up on top of the dessert.
5. Serve chilled with caramel sauce.

CHOCOLATE-SAFFRON CAKE WITH NUTMEG CRUNCH

NEW YORK SWEETS

STREUSEL

1 cup sugar
1 ⅔ cups almond flour
1 ⅔ cups all purpose flour
2 sticks unsalted butter, cold
and cut into ½-inch cubes

1. Mix the sugar, almond flour, and all purpose flour in a mixing bowl.
2. Add the cold butter and cut the butter in until it has the texture of coarse cornmeal.
3. Place on a parchment lined baking pan, and bake at 350° until golden in color, approximately 15 to 20 minutes.
4. Cool and set aside.

SAFFRON ICE CREAM

½ tsp. saffron
2 cups milk
½ cup heavy cream
4 tsp. powdered milk
5 egg yolks
3 Tbsp. glucose powder
2 Tbsp. honey
½ tsp. ice cream
⅓ cup sugar

1. In a medium saucepan, mix saffron with milk and cream and warm up to 122°.
2. Add milk powder, yolks, dry glucose, and honey. Mix well.
3. Combine stabilizer with the sugar and add it to the liquid using a whisk.
4. Cook this mixture to 183°.
5. Pasteurize and let rest for one night in the refrigerator.
6. Pour through a fine mesh strainer and process in an ice cream machine according to manufacturer's directions.

FOUR SEASONS
Hotels and Resorts

EXECUTIVE PASTRY CHEF
Luis Robledo-Richards

CHOCOLATE CREAM

2 cups heavy cream
¼ cup sugar
3 egg yolks
11 ounces 40% milk
chocolate, finely chopped

1. In a sauce pan, bring the cream and sugar to a boil over medium heat.
2. Whisk the yolks to break them up and gradually whisk in some of the hot cream into the yolks.
3. Whisk yolk mixture back into remaining hot cream and cook over low heat until it begins to coat the back of a spoon, approximately 3 minutes.
4. Pour through a fine mesh strainer over the chopped chocolate and emulsify with a hand held blender.
5. Let set in the refrigerator over night.

SAFFRON CREAM WITH CARAMEL

¼ tsp. saffron
½ cup milk
1 ¾ cups heavy cream
4 gelatin sheets
½ cup sugar
5 egg yolks

1. In a small saucepan, mix saffron, milk and cream and warm up to 122°.
2. Let stand for 20 minutes.
3. Place the sheets of gelatin in ice cold water to soften and set aside.
4. In a heavy-bottomed saucepan, cook the sugar to a blonde caramel color.
5. Once sugar has caramelized, remove from the heat and carefully add the hot saffron cream, stirring until well combined.
6. Add the egg yolks and cook to 183°.
7. Remove gelatin from ice water, squeezing out excess liquid and add it to the hot cream mixture.
8. Pour through a fine mesh strainer and chill overnight.

SAFFRON CARAMEL SAUCE

1 ¾ cups sugar
1 cup water
¼ tsp. saffron
Juice of one lemon

1. In a heavy-bottomed saucepan, over medium heat, cook the sugar to a blonde caramel color.
2. Remove from the heat and carefully add all of the water, stirring until well combined.
3. Add the saffron and the lemon juice.
4. Pour through a fine mesh strainer and cool.

NUTMEG SUGAR TUILE

7 oz. white fondant
⅔ cup glucose
¼ tsp. freshly ground nutmeg

1. Cook fondant and glucose to 330°.
2. Add fresh nutmeg and pour onto a silpat.
3. When it cools down, grind this sugar to a fine powder using a food processor.
4. Sprinkle the powder on a silpat and bake at 300° for 2 minutes. Remove from silpat immediately.
5. Let cool and keep in a dry place until ready to use.

ASSEMBLY

1. In a small cake ring, make a thin base with the streusel.
2. In a pastry bag fitted with a ½" plain tip, pipe some of the chocolate cream on top of the streusel.
3. Let set in the refrigerator for 15 minutes.
4. Add a layer of saffron cream over the chocolate cream and let set in the refrigerator for 1 hour.
5. Finish by adding some more chocolate cream and freeze for 2 hours.
6. Unmold and spray with chocolate
7. Place a chocolate saffron cake on a plate and make a quenelle of saffron ice cream.
8. Delicately decorate with a nutmeg tuile and some of the saffron caramel sauce.

RICOTTA FRITTERS

craft

PASTRY CHEF
Karen DeMasco

FILLING
1 lb. ricotta
⅓ cup sugar
Zest of one lemon

1. In a bowl, mix ricotta, sugar, and lemon zest. Chill one hour.
2. Using a small ice cream scoop, drop balls onto a parchment or foil-lined cookie sheet.
3. Freeze until solid.

DOUGH
4 cups all purpose flour
½ cup plus 2 Tbsp. sugar
2 Tbsp. baking powder
Pinch freshly grated nutmeg
Zest of one lemon
2 tsp. salt
8 eggs
½ cup honey
1 tsp. vanilla extract
1 lb. ricotta

1. In a bowl, whisk flour, sugar, baking powder, nutmeg, lemon zest, and salt.
2. In a separate bowl, whisk eggs, honey, and vanilla extract.
3. Make a well in the flour mixture and slowly pour in the egg mixture. Mix until combined.
4. Fold in the ricotta.
5. Roll the dough out between sheets of parchment paper to ¼" thick and then freeze for several hours.
6. Once frozen, cut dough into 2" circles using a round cutter.
7. Sandwich one ball of filling between two discs of dough.
8. As the dough begins to thaw, form it into a ball, pinching the edges as you go.
9. Refrigerate until you are ready to fry.

CINNAMON SUGAR
1 cup superfine sugar
1 Tbsp. ground cinnamon
¼ tsp. cardamom
Pinch of salt

1. In a bowl, mix sugar, cinnamon, cardamom, and salt together. Set aside.

ASSEMBLY
1 qt. canola oil

1. Fill saucepan with 4" of oil and heat to 390°.
2. Carefully place a couple of fritters into hot oil and fry for approximately 3 minutes until dark golden brown, making sure to flip so they brown evenly.
3. Toss warm fritters in cinnamon sugar.

BUTTERSCOTCH PANNA COTTA

SERVES 6

20 oz. (1 lb., 4oz.) butterscotch candy, crushed

9 cups heavy cream

½ vanilla bean, split and scraped

6 ½ sheets gelatin

1. Un-wrap butterscotch candies. Place candies in a zip lock bag and crush candies either with the bottom of a pot or a rolling pin until they resemble small pebbles. This will facilitate the melting process.
2. Place crushed butterscotch candies into a pot with heavy cream and vanilla bean. Slowly bring to a boil over a low flame, insuring that the candies are completely melted.
3. Soak sheets of gelatin in cold water until they become soft. Remove softened sheets from water and squeeze out the excess water. Place gelatin leaves in hot cream base and stir until the leaves have dissolved.
4. Strain the panna cotta base through a mesh strainer and pour into martini glasses. Refrigerate overnight.
5. The following day, top the panna cotta with the melted curry jelly (recipe below). This needs to be done at least 4 hours in advance so the jelly can set up and become firm.

CURRY JELLY

1 cup water

½ cup sugar

¼ tsp. gelatin powder

1 ½ Tbsp. madras curry powder

1. Lightly toast madras curry in a sauté pan over a low flame for about 3 ½ minutes. Make sure to stir curry around with a wooden spoon to avoid burning. Remove from flame and set aside.
2. Combine 2 tablespoons of granulated sugar with the gelatin powder to prevent the powder from lumping up.
3. Place water, sugar, gelatin mix and the toasted curry into a pot large enough to hold everything.
4. Bring to a boil over a medium flame in order to dissolve both the sugar and the gelatin.
5. Strain jelly through a fine mesh strainer and either store in an airtight plastic container or cool to a point where it is still pourable, and top panna cotta in martini glasses that have been allowed to set overnight.
6. Refrigerate for 4 hours to allow jelly to set up.
7. If you are using this jelly the next day, place jelly in the microwave on a low setting in order to melt it. Set the timer for a 15 second intervals, the jelly should feel no warmer than your body's temperature.

davidburke & donatella

EXECUTIVE CHEF
David Burke

BLACK AND WHITE NAPOLEON

MAKES 6 TO 8 NAPOLEONS

SHORTBREAD PASTRY

7 Tbsp. unsalted butter,
room temperature
½ cup brown sugar
1 orange, finely grated zest
Pinch of salt
1¾ cups all purpose flour
½ tsp. baking powder
1 egg yolk
1½ tsp. milk

1. In a standing mixer, fitted with the paddle attachment, combine the butter, sugar, orange zest, salt, flour, and baking powder and beat until combined.
2. Beat in eggs and milk.
3. Refrigerate for 1 hour.
4. Preheat oven to 350º.
5. Split the dough in half and roll each half as thin as possible.
6. Place each onto a parchment lined 12 x 18 pan.
7. Bake for 8 to 10 minutes or until golden brown.

PASTRY CHEF
Jasmine Bojic

PASSION FRUIT MOUSSE FILLING

⅔ cup passion fruit pulp
2 Tbsp. sugar
½ tsp. NH pectin
(available in specialty stores)
1 cup single cream 35%

1. Warm the passion fruit pulp in a small saucepan over low heat until lukewarm.
2. Add the sugar and pectin. Mix together and bring to a boil.
3. Remove from heat, place in a bowl, cover, and refrigerate overnight.
4. Using a standing mixer mixer, whip the cream until thick and stiff.
5. Gently fold in the cooled passion fruit mixture, using a rubber spatula.
6. Set aside.

MUSCOVADO JELLY

½ cup muscovado sugar
(dark brown sugar available in specialty stores)
1¼ cups lukewarm water
¾ tsp. agar-agar powder
(available in specialty stores)
2 tsp. light brown sugar
4 tsp. lemon juice

1. In a small sauce pan, melt the muscovado sugar with the lukewarm water.
2. Mix the agar-agar powder with the sugar.
3. Add the lemon juice to the melted moscovado sugar and then add the agar-agar to the brown sugar mixture.
4. Bring to a boil, stirring constantly.
5. Pour into a square glass dish.
6. Cover and allow to jell in the refrigerator overnight.

CHOCOLATE CREAM

$^1/_2$ cup heavy cream

$^1/_2$ cup milk

3 egg yolks

2 Tbsp. sugar

4 oz. Pur Caraibe chocolate 66%
(available in specialty stores)

1. Scald the cream and milk over moderate heat in a small saucepan.
2. In a separate bowl, whisk together the egg yolks and sugar until lemon colored.
3. Whisk some of the hot cream into egg yolk mixture. Whisk egg yolk mixture back into cream mixture. Over low heat, stir constantly with a wooden spoon until the custard has thickened enough to coat the back of the spoon.
4. Pass through a strainer and return to a clean saucepan and keep warm.
5. Place the chocolate in a bowl and melt over a pot of simmering water.
6. Add the chocolate to the custard and mix in thoroughly, using a rubber spatula to obtain a smooth and glossy texture.
7. Cover and refrigerate.

ASSEMBLY

1. Crack the dough into large pieces (about 2" by 6").
2. Place one piece of dough on a plate.
3. Using a pastry bag fitted with a $^1/_2$-inch plain tip, pipe $^1/_8$th of the passion fruit mousse on top.
4. Place a second layer of dough on top of the passion fruit mousse.
5. Using another pastry bag fitted with a $^1/_2$-inch tip, pipe $^1/_8$th of the chocolate cream on that layer.
6. Top with another layer of dough to form a triple layer napoleon.
7. Stand the napoleon on its side. Cut the jelly into rectangular shapes and use one on each side of the napoleon to hold it up.

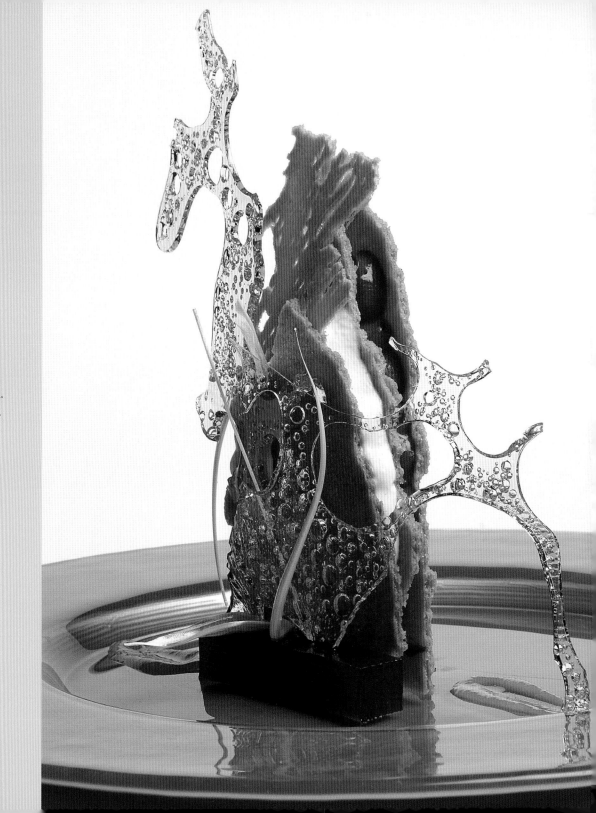

Milk Chocolate Mousse Cake, Raisin Compote, and Autumn Spice Ice Cream

Pumpkin Biscuit

1 cup all purpose flour
½ tsp. powdered cinnamon
½ tsp. baking soda
2 large eggs
1 ¼ cups granulated sugar
1 cup pumpkin puree, fresh or canned

1. Sift together the flour, cinnamon and baking soda and set aside.
2. On a mixer fitted with the whisk attachment, whip the eggs with the sugar for approximately 5 minutes, until thick and pale yellow.
3. Add the pumpkin puree to the eggs and mix to combine.
4. Fold the dry ingredients into the egg/pumpkin mixture.
5. Pour onto a greased 9 x 13-inch pan.
6. Bake at 350° until a light golden color and cake springs back when lightly touched.
7. Unmold the cake immediately and let cool.

Raisin Compote

1 ¼ cups water
¾ cups sugar
1 vanilla bean
Juice of one lemon
¾ cup golden raisins
¾ cup raisins

1. Combine all ingredients in a sauce pan.
2. Bring to a simmer and cook until raisins are tender and plump.
3. Remove vanilla bean, cool and refrigerate.

db
bistro moderne

Pastry Chef
Michael Brock

Autumn Spice Ice Cream

1 pt. milk
1 pt. heavy cream
3/4 cup sugar, divided
2 cinnamon sticks
2 star anise
8 allspice
5 whole cloves
A pinch of fresh nutmeg
8 egg yolks

1. Combine the milk, cream, half of the sugar and all of the spices in a sauce pan and bring to a boil over medium heat.
2. Turn off heat and let mixture stand for 20 minutes.
3. Strain the spices and bring milk mixture back to a boil.
4. In a separate bowl, whisk together the yolks and the remaining sugar.
5. While whisking the yolks, slowly add some of the hot milk mixture, until yolks are warm.
6. Slowly whisk the yolk mixture back into the remaining milk mixture and cook over low heat stirring constantly until it gently coats the back of the spoon.
7. Strain through a fine mesh strainer and cool down immediately over an ice bath.
8. Process in an ice cream machine according to the manufacturer's instructions.

Pumpkin Anglaise

1 cup milk
1 cup heavy cream
Pinch of salt
1 split vanilla bean
4 egg yolks
⅓ cup sugar
⅓ cup pumpkin puree

1. Combine the milk, cream, salt, and split and scraped vanilla bean in a sauce pan and bring to a boil over medium heat.
2. Whisk together the sugar and the egg yolks.
3. While whisking the yolks, slowly add some of the hot milk mixture, until yolks are warm.
4. Slowly whisk the yolk mixture back into the remaining milk mixture and cook over low heat stirring constantly until it gently coats the back of the spoon.
5. Add the pumpkin puree immediately and blend with an emulsion blender.
6. Strain through a fine mesh strainer and chill immediately.

Milk Chocolate Mousse Cake

1 ½ cups heavy cream
2 tablespoons sugar
2 yolks
⅓ cup heavy cream
4 ounces milk chocolate

1. In a standing mixer fitted with a whip attachment, whip the larger amount of heavy cream until it begins to hold its shape. Refrigerate until ready to use.
2. Combine sugar, yolks, and remaining heavy cream in a bowl over a pot of simmering water and whisk constantly until hot and thick, approximately 10 minutes.
3. Pour into the bowl of an electric mixer and whip cool with whisk attachment.
4. Place the milk chocolate in a bowl over the pot of boiling water and melt, being careful not to let the chocolate get too hot.
5. Add half of the whipped cream to the melted chocolate and whisk vigorously so the mixture doesn't seize.
6. Fold in the remaining whipped cream until just combined.
7. Gently fold the yolk mixture into the chocolate whipped cream, folding carefully, as not to lose any volume.

Assembly

1. Place the pumpkin biscuit back into a 9 x 13 x 2 inch pan.
2. Add the mousse and spread evenly with a cake spatula.
3. Freeze until set and then cut into rectangular shapes and place them on plates.
5. Garnish with some of the raisin compote, pumpkin anglaise and a scoop of the autumn spice ice cream.

TROPICAL TASTING PLATE

SAVARIN
8 oz. bread flour
4 eggs
Pinch of salt
1 oz. sugar
½ oz. fresh yeast
1 oz. water
2 oz. butter, cold
Zest of 2 limes

1. Combine the first 6 ingredients and mix with the paddle attachment until the dough pulls away from the sides of the bowl.
2. Add the butter and the zest and mix until incorporated.
3. Let the dough rest at room temperature for 15 minutes.
4. Fill small Savarin molds and let proof.
5. Bake at 350° for 25 minutes.

SYRUP
1 cup sugar
2 cups water
Juice of 4 limes

1. Combine ingredients and bring to a boil.
2. Completely soak the Savarins.

COUS-COUS
3.5 oz. cous-cous
3.5 oz. water
2 oz. coconut milk
2 oz. coco lopez
2 oz. sugar

1. Combine all the ingredients in a small saucepot and bring to a boil.
2. Reduce the heat to a simmer and let cook until all the liquid is absorbed, approximately 10 minutes.

FRUIT
1ea. banana, mango, papaya
5 strawberries
¼ pineapple
2 passion fruits
2 star fuits
Zest and juice of 2 limes

1. Finely dice the fruit and mix together with the lime juice and zest and let marinate.
2. When cous-cous is cooled, mix the fruit in.

STRAWBERRY JUNIPER SAUCE
1 pt. strawberries
2 juniper berries
10 oz. Grenadine
3.5 oz. sugar

1. Combine everything and boil for 2 minutes.

COCONUT SORBET
2 eans coco lopez
1 qt. milk

1. Mix together and freeze in ice cream machine.

PATE A BRIC
2oz. butter
2 oz. sugar

1. Butter and sugar both sides of the Pate a Bric.
2. Cut into triangles and place between 2 sheet pans.
3. Bake at 350° until golden brown, approximately 5 minutes.

COCONUT PASSION FRUIT NAPOLEON
4 oz. egg whites
6 oz. sugar
3 oz. unsweetened coconut, shredded
4.5 oz. passion fruit puree
3 oz. sugar
4 oz. butter
4 egg yolks
1 gelatin sheet
¼ cup heavy cream

1. Make a French meringue with egg whites and 6 ounces of sugar. Whip until stiff peak.
2. Fold in the coconut.
3. Pipe into small discs and let dry in the oven on 200° for 2 hours.
4. Make a curd with the passion fruit puree, 3 ounces of sugar, butter, and egg yolks, by combining them and cooking them over a double boiler until mixture reaches 160°.
5. Add the gelatin while curd is still hot. Let cool.
6. Whip the cream and fold it into the curd.
7. Layer this between the discs.
8. Garnish with toasted coconut, passion fruit seeds, and a mango rose.

The
French
Culinary Institute
NEW YORK CITY

DIRECTOR OF PASTRY ARTS
Tina Casaceli

Hazelnut or Almond Raspberry Tart

SERVES 8

TARTS

1 cup unsalted butter, softened
1 cup plus 2 Tbsp. sugar
8 oz. almond or hazelnut paste
6 large eggs
1 tsp. vanilla
1 cup cake flour
1 tsp. baking powder
1 cup lemon curd (recipe follows)
2 pints fresh raspberries
Confectioners' sugar

1. In an electric mixer fitted with a paddle attachment, cream butter and sugar until light.
2. Add the paste and mix until smooth.
3. Add one egg at a time, mixing well after each addition. Add vanilla.
4. Sift flour and baking powder and fold into wet ingredients.
5. Place 3-inch flan rings on 1/2 sheet pan lined with parchment.
6. Spray with non-stick spray.
7. Spoon batter into prepared flan rings and bake at 375°F for approximately 18 minutes.
8. Let cool in molds and then slice into three equal layers.
9. Fold whipped cream into 1 cup of lemon curd.
10. Place one layer of cake on a plate and spoon a tablespoon of lemon curd cream on top. Place raspberries in a concentric circle on top of lemon curd cream using about 10 raspberries. Cover with second layer and repeat with lemon curd cream and raspberries.
11. Place third and final layer on top and dust with confectioners' sugar and decorate the plate with raspberries.

LEMON CURD CREAM

12 egg yolks
1 cup sugar
1 cup lemon juice
2 sticks butter
Zest of 2 lemons
½ cup heavy cream

1. In a bowl, whisk together yolks, sugar, and lemon juice.
2. Cook over a pot of simmering water for ten minutes, stirring frequently.
3. When the mixture is thickened, whisk in the butter.
4. Strain through a fine mesh strainer and stir in zest.
5. Chill until cooled.
6. In a separate bowl whip the heavy cream until stiff and fold into the cooled lemon curd.

MAROONS

EXECUTIVE CHEF
Patricia Williams

PLUM SOUP WITH ALMOND-MASCARPONE CREAM

NEW YORK SWEETS

SERVES 4

PLUM SOUP
2 cups water
1 vanilla bean, split open
½ cup sugar
6 Santa Rosa plums, cut into 8 pieces ea.

1. Bring water, vanilla bean, and sugar to a boil in a medium saucepan. Stir to dissolve sugar.
2. Add plums and simmer on low until fruit is hot throughout but still retains its shape.
3. Let cool and refrigerate overnight.
4. The next day, pour soup through a fine mesh strainer, discard solids and refrigerate until serving.

ALMOND MASCARPONE CREAM
1 cup heavy cream
4 oz. almond paste
2 Tbsp. sugar
2 bitter almonds, if you have it
⅓ cup Mascarpone

1. Put cream, almond paste, sugar and bitter almonds in a small pot and bring to a boil over medium heat, stirring to melt sugar and almond paste.
2. Let cool. Refrigerate overnight.
3. The next day, strain cream through a strainer lined with cheesecloth.
4. Put strained cream in cold bowl of standing mixer fitted with the whisk attachment. Add the Mascarpone and whip until medium peaks form.
5. Refrigerate until serving.

PHYLLO LACE COOKIES
1 pkg. phyllo dough, frozen
3 oz. butter, melted
2 Tbsp. sugar

1. Take out frozen phyllo dough from freezer. Unwrap plastic from dough and cut down through the roll into ¼" slices. Continue cutting about ⅓ of the roll, then wrap the rest up and return to freezer.
2. Separate the phyllo dough strands as best as you can into a bowl.
3. Sprinkle with sugar and then pour the melted butter over it. Toss to coat.
4. Put the tangle of phyllo between 2 silpat sheets and roll with a rolling pin into 1 layer, about ⅛" thick. Or put the tangle between two pieces of parchment paper (cut to fit a sheet pan) and roll. Transfer with both sheets of parchment to a sheet pan and place another sheet pan on top.
5. Bake at 350° for about 10 minutes, until golden.
6. Halfway through the baking, take the sheet pan out, carefully lift the silpat on top and cut into 2½" round cookies with a cookie cutter. Return to the oven to finish baking. Let cool.

le Zie 2000

TRATTORIA

PASTRY CHEF
Maria Lindstrand

TO SERVE
Ladle the soup into 4 shallow bowls. Sprinkle some match stick cut plums into each bowl and make a small fan of sliced plums for the middle. Carefully lay the phyllo cookie on top of fanned slices and place a quenelle of almond cream on top. Follow with one more cookie and garnish with plum slices cut thin on a mandolin and sprinkle with lemon thyme.

Fig Carpaccio

Syrup
1 bottle ruby port
¾ cup sugar
1 zest of lemon

1. Combine port, sugar and lemon rind with no pith (white inside layer) in a pot, bring to a slow boil and reduce to ⅕ of the volume.
2. Let cool and reserve

Carpaccio
2 lb. fresh figs
Juice from 2 lemons
1 Tbsp. cinnamon powder
¾ cup maple sugar

1. Wash figs and cut in half lengthwise. Fillet out the center of each fig. Discard the skin or add them to the jam for the ice cream.
2. Combine all ingredients with the fig fillets and place on a cutting board and chop until completely smooth. Avoid doing it with a food processor because the blades cut it too quickly.
3. Place ¼ of this puree onto the center of a plate. Gently cover the entire plate with a square of plastic wrap, but do not pull it tight. Using a wide round pot, press out the figs so it forms a thin round. Repeat this 3 more times with the rest of the puree.
4. Reserve with plastic on top until ready to use.

Madeleine Sponge Cake
1⅛ cups sugar
8 eggs
1½ cups flour
1 Tbsp. cinnamon powder

1. Combine sugar and eggs and whisk until triple in volume.
2. Fold in flour and cinnamon until evenly incorporated.
3. Pipe into very lightly greased madeleine molds and bake at 375° for 8 to 10 minutes, until golden brown.

PASTRY CHEF
David Carmichael

Ice Cream
2 cups heavy cream
1⅛ cups sugar
2 cinnamon sticks
3 star anise
14 egg yolks
2 cups crème fraiche

1. Combine heavy cream, sugar, and spices in a pot.
2. Over medium-high heat, bring the liquid to just shy of a boil, lower the heat until cream is barely simmering. Simmer for 5 minutes.
3. Strain, return to pot, and heat again to just boiling.
4. Whisk yolks until smooth.
5. Temper the hot cream into the egg yolks by adding 1/4 of the cream to the yolks in a steady stream, while whisking continuously.
6. Return pot to the heat, whisk in the yolk mixture, and cook for 2 minutes while stirring gently with a wooden spoon.
7. Strain into a clean bowl and allow to cool. Once cool, whisk in the crème fraiche.
8. Spin in ice cream machine according to manufacturer's instructions.
9. Once the ice cream is ready, extract into frozen mixing bowl and let set in the freezer while you prepare the fig jam.

Fig Jam
1 lb. figs
¼ cup lemon juice

1. Wash and remove the stems from the figs.
2. Lightly crush the figs and place in a pot, along with the lemon juice.
3. Cook on medium heat until the figs are completely broken down, approximately 15 to 20 minutes.
4. Puree in a food processor until very smooth, being careful not to incorporate any air.
5. Cool and then cut into (don't mix) ice cream to produce a swirl effect.
6. Transfer to an appropriate container and freeze for 1 hour or more.

Vanilla Tuile
8 oz. egg whites
¾ cup plus 1 Tbsp. powdered sugar
Seeds of 1 vanilla bean, split open and scraped out seeds
8 oz. (2 sticks) butter, melted
1 cup flour

1. Combine egg whites, sugar, and vanilla bean in a bowl over a double boiler and whisk until sugar is completely dissolved.
2. Whisk in melted butter and flour until smooth and let rest in refrigerator for 1 to 2 hours.
3. Using a pastry bag and a small round pastry tip, pipe the batter onto a cookie sheet lined with parchment paper into random, wacky shapes.
4. Cook for approximately 5 minutes until golden brown. Remove while hot and then shape into a loose ball.

CHOCOLATE AND BANANA TORTE
MACADAMIA NUT ICE CREAM AND BANANA CARAMEL

CHOCOLATE AND BANANA TORTE
Yields 5 - 4 oz. cakes

4 oz. butter, unsalted
4 ¾ oz. bittersweet chocolate
1 egg
3 egg yolks
2 Tbsp. sugar
½ cup macadamia nuts, toasted
1 cup bananas, chopped

1. Preheat the oven to 350º.
2. Separately melt the butter and chocolate and cool slightly.
3. Whisk eggs and sugar (don't beat air into the mix).
4. Alternately stir the butter and chocolate into the egg mixture.
5. Add bananas and nuts.
6. Pour into 5 molds that are sprayed with non-stick cooking spray and coated with sugar.
7. Bake for 10 minutes. Reserve.

BANANA CARAMEL SAUCE
Yields 1 cup

1 cup sugar
3 Tbsp. lemon juice
1 banana

1. In a saucepan, mix the sugar and lemon juice together to form "wet sand".
2. Over medium high heat, heat without stirring until it makes a light caramel.
3. Lower heat to medium, add banana and cook three minutes.
4. Stir and strain. Cool.

BANANA CHIPS
Yields 5 – 8 chips

2 ripe bananas
2 tsp. super fine sugar
2 tsp. tapioca flour

1. Puree the bananas with the lemon juice.
2. Spread out the puree on sheet pan lined with a silpat mat or parchment paper (using a template for desired shape) or free form individual chips to desired shape.
3. Sprinkle the top with sugar and tapioca flour.
4. Bake at 200º for 2 hours. This slowly dries the chips.
5. Remove from oven and while still warm and soft, shape to encircle the individual cakes, removed from molds. Cool.

CHARLIE PALMER'S
MÉTRAZUR

EXECUTIVE CHEF
Michael Lockhard

MACADAMIA NUT ICE CREAM

Yields 1 cup

⅓ cup macadamia nuts

1 cup heavy cream

6 oz. milk

3 oz. sugar

1 vanilla bean, split
and seeds scraped

3 egg yolks

1. Lightly toast the macadamia nuts.
2. Combine the nuts, heavy cream, milk, sugar, and vanilla bean and scald by heating to just below the boiling point.
3. In a separate bowl, whisk yolks lightly.
4. Temper into yolks by adding ¼ of the cream mixture into the yolks while whisking constantly.
5. Return pan to heat, and add yolks.
6. Stir with a rubber spatula until nape consistency (when a line is left after running finger over spatula).
7. Puree in a blender or food processor and strain through a chinoise.
8. Cool in an ice bath by pouring mixture into a clean bowl set on top of a bowl of ice.
9. Stir occasionally to cool.
10. Freeze in an ice cream machine.

SUGAR COATED MACADAMIA NUTS

Yields ½ cup

½ cup macadamia nuts

2 oz. sugar

1 oz. water

1. Toast the nuts on a cookie sheet in a 300º oven for 5-7 minutes. Watch carefully.
2. In a saucepan, boil water and sugar to 237º to 240º (softball stage).
3. Add nuts and stir in to coat.
4. Cool on a silpat (silicone) mat or sheet pan. Reserve.

PEACH AND AMARETTI COBBLER WITH PEACH ICE CREAM

SERVES 4

PEACH ICE CREAM

2 cups milk

2 cups heavy cream

1 cup sugar

8 egg yolks

10 fresh peaches, juiced
(this should make approx.
6 – 8 oz. of juice)

1. Bring milk, cream, peach juice and ½ cup sugar to boil.
2. Combine the egg yolks with the remaining sugar and whisk until thoroughly incorporated and thick.
3. Temper the yolk mixture by pouring half of the hot cream mixture into the yolks, whisking constantly and then return the yolk mixture back into the hot cream. Continue to cook over low heat stirring constantly for 3 to 5 minutes. Don't bring back to a boil.
4. Strain, pour into a bowl and cool down over an ice bath.
5. Spin the ice cream according to the directions for the type of ice cream machine you are using.

FILLING

4 peaches, peeled and cut
into ¼ inch slices

2 Tbsp. sugar

1 Tbsp. flour

1 Tbsp. amaretto or almond extract

1. Combine filling ingredients in large bowl, tossing gently until well mixed.
2. Spread evenly in a 9 x 9 baking dish.

TOPPING

¾ cup flour

½ cup light brown sugar

¼ cup sugar

1 tsp. cinnamon

½ cup blanched almonds,
toasted and coarsely chopped

8 Tbsp. unsalted butter, cut
into ½ inch pieces and chilled

1. In a food processor, pulse together the flour, brown sugar, sugar, and cinnamon until well mixed.
2. Add the almonds and pulse until the nuts are in small pieces.
3. Add the pieces of butter and pulse until the butter is finely broken up.
4. Continue to pulse until the topping no longer looks sandy and is just beginning to hold together.

ASSEMBLY

1 cup mini amaretti cookies

1. Preheat the oven to 375°.
2. Distribute the topping evenly over the peaches.
3. Add the amaretti cookies.
4. Bake for 30 to 40 minutes, until the edges are bubbling.

Note – Lay a sheet of aluminum foil on the rack below the cobbler while it is cooking to catch the drippings.

The Sea Grill

PASTRY CHEF

Jane Ebert

Summer Sundae

NEW YORK SWEETS

SERVES 4

GELEE ELDERFLOWER
2 gelatin sheets
1 cup elderflower soda

1. Set gelatin leaves in a bowl of ice water and set aside to soften.
2. In a saucepan heat 2 tablespoons of elderflower soda and add the softened gelatin. Continue cooking over low heat until gelatin is melted.
3. Once completely melted, incorporate the melted gelatin mixture back into the remaining elderflower soda.
4. Pour approximately ¼ cup of the gelee into four serving glasses and refrigerate to set.

APRICOT MARMALADE
2 ¼ pounds fresh apricots
1 cup sugar
1 teaspoon Pectin NH
Juice of one lemon
1 vanilla bean, split and scraped

1. Half and pit the fresh apricots.
2. Mix the pectin and sugar together.
3. Place apricots, sugar, lemon juice, and vanilla seeds in a saucepan and cook on low heat until thickened. Set aside to cool.
4. Place a layer of marmalade approximately ¾" high on top of gelee.

CURRANT JUICE
1 lb. fresh red currants
¾ cup sugar

1. Mix the currants and sugar together and place in a saucepan.
2. Cook over medium heat until the skins burst from the fruit.
3. Remove the fruit from the heat and strain the currants through a fine mesh strainer.
4. Refrigerate to cool.

PEACHES
1 ½ cups sugar
4 cups water
Juice of 2 lemons
4 peaches

1. In a large saucepan, bring the sugar, water and lemon juice to a boil over medium heat.
2. Once boiling, drop the peaches into the syrup and remove the pot from the heat and allow the peaches to cool in their own syrup.
3. Periodically check the texture of the peach. Once a knife can easily penetrate the entire peach to the pit, place the peaches and syrup on an ice bath.
4. Store the peaches in the syrup until ready to use.

PEACHES SORBET
1 ¼ cups water
1 ¼ cups sugar
60 gr. glucose powder
½ pound cooked peaches
3 cups Cerdon

1. In a saucepan, bring the water, sugar and glucose powder to a boil to make a syrup. Refrigerate.
2. Pit the peaches cooked in recipe above.
3. Once the syrup from step one has cooled, puree the cooked peaches and cooled syrup together.
4. Incorporate the Cerdon and churn in an ice cream machine and freeze according to manufacturer's directions.

CARAMELIZED ALMONDS
4 cups water
5 ¼ cups sugar
Almond batons

1. Place the water and sugar together in a saucepan and bring to a boil over medium heat to make a syrup.
2. Place the almonds in a mixing bowl.
3. Pour the syrup over the almonds and let soak for approximately 1 hour.
4. Strain the almonds and transfer them to a sheet pan to air dry for approximately 20 minutes.
5. Bake at 300º for 6 minutes or until light caramel color.

PASTRY CHEF
Franck Labasse

FRIED ICE CREAM

FRIED ICE CREAM
Wonder white bread
Vanilla bean ice cream

1. Trim off bread crusts. Place a scoop of ice cream between bread and mold into a ball, making sure to seal edges together. Plastic wrap each and freeze until hard.
2. Add enough oil to be about 3 inches deep in pot. If you are using an electric wok, set it on 400°. Otherwise, put heat on medium to medium high temperature. Fry until nicely brown. Don't brown too quickly. Fry one at a time.

RASPBERRY SAUCE
1 bag frozen red raspberries
2 cups sugar
1 cup cream de cassis
Salt

1. Mix all ingredients in a saucepot, over low flame until fruit is soft.

Siam Inn

EXECUTIVE CHEF
Tanaporn Tangwibulchai

KEY LIME ALASKA

LEMON CAKE

6 cups cake flour
2 Tbsp. baking powder
1 tsp. salt
2 ¼ cups (4 1/2 sticks) butter
4 cups sugar
Zest of 6 lemons
10 eggs
2 ½ cups heavy cream
2 Tbsp. vanilla extract

1. Stir together flour, baking powder, and salt. Set aside.
2. In a mixer, cream butter, sugar, and zest until fluffy.
3. Add eggs, one at a time, until completely incorporated.
4. In a separate bowl, combine cream and vanilla extract. Set aside.
5. Slowly, and in thirds, add in dry ingredients, alternating with the wet (heavy cream), just until all ingredients are incorporated.
6. Line a half pan sheet (12 x 18) with parchment paper, then grease and flour.
7. Fill pan no more than ¾ full.
8. Bake at 350° until golden brown.
9. Cool completely and chill overnight. Place in the freezer until slightly frozen before slicing.

BRANDIED FRUIT

½ cup each of raspberries, blueberries, strawberries and blackberries,
½ cup sugar
1 cup brandy

1. Toss fruit with sugar.
2. Put in a large pan over medium-high heat for 30 seconds.
3. Add brandy and ignite, being careful to keep your distance.
4. Let all the alcohol cook out.
5. Strain and set aside.

STRIP HOUSE

EXECUTIVE PASTRY CHEF
SARAH BETH SHERER

KEY LIME ICE CREAM

1 cup milk
1 ½ cups heavy cream
3 Tbsp. lime zest
¾ cup sugar
Pinch of salt
6 egg yolks
⅔ cup key lime juice

1. In a large pot, combine milk, heavy cream, and zest. Bring to a boil.
2. In a large bowl, whisk together yolks and sugar.
3. Slowly temper milk into yolks by adding ¼ of the milk while whisking constantly. Then return the pot to the heat and add the yolks while whisking constantly.
4. Stir continuously and gently with a wooden spoon until a line is left on the back of the spoon when you run your finger over it.
5. Remove from heat and add lime juice.
6. Strain through a fine sieve into a clean bowl resting in an ice bath
7. Let mixture cool completely while stirring occasionally.
8. Process in ice cream machine according to manufacturer's instructions.

SWISS MERINGUE

1 ½ cups egg whites
1 ½ cups sugar
2 Tbsp. lemon juice

1. Place egg whites and sugar in a bowl and heat over a pan of simmering water. Whisk gently until the sugar dissolves completely (there should be no gritty feeling when you rub some of the mixture between your thumb and index finger) and the egg whites are uniformly hot (about 130°)
2. Transfer the bowl from the pan to the mixer fitted with a whip or use a hand mixer. Whip on medium speed until the meringue is cool and increased in volume. Swiss meringue should be stiff, but not dry.
3. Fill pastry bag, fitted with a star tip, with the meringue.
4. Try to use immediately.

ASSEMBLY

Fresh mint leaves
Powdered sugar

1. After the cake is slightly frozen, remove cake from pan and slice into two equal layers and set aside.
2. Overlap pan with saran wrap and replace bottom layer of cake.
3. Spread ice cream evenly onto the bottom layer and place top layer over ice cream.
4. Wrap the saran wrap up and over the cake to ensure no leakage. Let freeze.
5. When cake is frozen, cut into 3" x 3" squares and cut on a bias. Place on a plate.
6. Using previously filled pastry bag, stream swiss meringue up one side, creating height. Brulee until brown with kitchen torch.
7. On opposite side of the plate, using a small ring mold, place your brandied fruit.
8. Garnish with mint and a little powdered sugar.

DULCE DE LECHE

KAHLUA SYRUP
1 cup water
1 cup sugar
7 Tbsp. Kahlua

1. Bring water and sugar to a boil.
2. Remove from heat.
3. Add the Kahlua and let cool.

DULCE DE LECHE MOUSSE
2 Tbsp (1 oz.) gelatin
1 cup cold water
6 ⅔ cups sugar
1 cup milk
2 cups cream
1 qt. whipped cream

1. Sprinkle the gelatin on the surface of a bowl with the cold water. Let sit until absorbed.
2. In a saucepan, over medium-high heat, cook the sugar until it caramelizes.
3. Remove from heat.
4. Carefully, while keeping distance, add the milk and cream, and then add the gelatin.
5. Let cool and then fold in the whipped cream.

PASTRY CHEF
Stephane Motir

CHOCOLATE SPONGE
7 egg yolks
½ cup water
½ cup oil
½ cup cake flour
¾ cup sugar
¼ cup cocoa powder
1 Tbsp. baking powder
Pinch of baking soda
8 egg whites
⅓ cup plus 1 Tbsp. sugar

1. Whip egg yolks, water and oil together in a bowl.
2. Sift together the cake flour, sugar, cocoa powder, baking powder, and baking soda and then add them to the egg mixture, mixing just until incorporated.
3. Whisk egg whites until they become foamy, then slowly add the sugar until it forms stiff peaks. Fold this meringue into the chocolate sponge mixture.
4. Pour onto a 12" x 18" sheet pan and bake at 350º for 7 to 10 minutes. Let cool.

COCONUT JOCONDE
12 egg whites, at room temperature
¾ cup 10x sugar
½ cup almond flour
¼ cup plus 1 Tbsp. shredded coconut
¼ cup flour
⅓ cup plus 1 Tbsp. sugar
3 eggs
1 ½ Tbsp. butter, melted

1. Preheat the oven to 425º.
2. Line sheet pan with parchment paper.
3. Make a meringue by beating the egg whites until frothy, then slowly adding sugar until stiff peaks form.
4. Mix all the remaining dry ingredients and the eggs together in a separate bowl.
5. Add the melted butter to this mixture.
6. Using a rubber spatula, gently fold in the meringue.
7. Place this batter into the pan and bake at 425º for 7 to 9 minutes, until lightly browned.
8. Remove from the pan and let cool.

ASSEMBLY
1. Line the sides of a pastry ring with the joconde sponge.
2. Put a circle of chocolate sponge on the bottom, brush it with Kahlua syrup, and add a little bit of dulce de leche mousse.
3. Repeat 3 times until you fill the ring up to the top.
4. Freeze.
5. Top the cake with a cold process glaze and with sprinkle coffee extract.
6. With a palate knife, smooth the top, creating a marble pattern.
7. Remove the pastry ring and decorate with a chocolate stencil.

TANGERINE PARFAIT

SERVES 8

TANGERINE SORBET
2 ½ cups tangerine juice
Zest of 2 tangerines
¼ cup lemon juice
¾ cup sugar
¼ cup corn syrup

1. Combine all ingredients well and store in the refrigerator overnight.
2. Strain, stir well, and pour into ice cream freezer.
3. Store sorbet in freezer until ready to use.

ALMOND CREMA
2 cups heavy cream
½ cup raw, blanched almonds
⅓ cup sugar
5 egg yolks
Pinch of salt
Almond extract to taste

1. Preheat oven to 350°.
2. Roast almonds for approximately 12 to 15 minutes.
3. In a small saucepan, heat cream to a simmer.
4. Grind almonds in a food processor while hot and add to hot cream.
5. Infuse for ½ hour and strain, reserving liquid and discarding solids.
6. Reheat almond cream with ½ of the sugar.
7. In a separate bowl, whisk egg yolks with the rest of the sugar.
8. Temper yolks by adding ¼ of the cream to the yolks while whisking constantly.
9. Add yolk mixture to cream and return saucepan to heat.
10. Cook over low heat, while gently stirring, until steam rises from the mixture (do not boil).
11. Strain custard into a clean bowl.
12. Cool in ice bath and stir occassionally.
13. Add a pinch of salt and ⅛ tsp of almond extract to taste.
14. Chill in refrigerator until ready to use.
15. Whisk by hand or with a mixer to lighten, similar to whipped cream when ready to serve.

enoteca
ŌTTŌ
pizzeria

PASTRY CHEF
Meredith Kurtzman

CRANBERRY GRANITA

1 ½ cups water

½ cup sugar

1 cup cranberries, fresh or frozen

Juice and zest of 1 orange

Juice of 1 lemon

1. Combine sugar and water in a small saucepan, simmer to dissolve sugar.

2. Add the cranberries and gently cook them for several minutes until they burst.

3. Cool mixture and puree in a food processor.

4. Strain through a fine sieve, saving the liquid, and discarding the solids.

5. Add orange juice, zest, and lemon juice.

6. Chill in a low, flat container in the freezer.

7. After 1 hour or so, scrape granita with a fork. Return to freezer and scrape every ½ hour until you have an evenly textured, flaky product.

8. Reserve in the freezer until you are ready to assemble the dessert.

ASSEMBLY

1. Pre-chill 8 glasses.

2. Spoon granita into the bottom of the glasses.

3. Scoop a ball of tangerine sorbet and drop into glass.

4. Spoon on some almond cream.

5. Serve immediately.

ROASTED PEAR WITH ORANGE CREAM FILLING AND ARMAGNAC SYRUP

SERVES 4

2 cups plus 2 Tbsp. sugar

7 Tbsp. corn syrup

½ cup cold water

1 ¾ cups hot water

4 ripe Bosc pears, peeled and cored

2 Tbsp. Armagnac

⅓ cup cream cheese

3 Tbsp. confectioners' sugar

2 Tbsp. butter, softened

Zest of 1 orange

1 ½ tsp. honey

1. Preheat oven to 350º

2. In a saucepan, combine the sugar, corn syrup, and enough of the cold water to melt the sugar. Cook until it turns a light caramel color, then add the hot water and stir until blended.

3. Place the pears in an ovenproof baking dish and pour the hot caramel over them.

4. Cover the baking dish with aluminum foil and bake in the oven until the pears are fork tender, about 45 minutes, basting the pears every 10 minutes.

5. When the pears are done, remove them from the caramel and place on a cooling rack. Reserve 1½ cups of the caramel and add the Armagnac. Set aside.

6. Mix together the cream cheese, sugar, butter, orange zest, and honey. Place the mixture in a pastry bag and pipe into the pears.

7. To serve, place each pear in a shallow bowl and sauce with the caramel syrup.

8. If desired, garnish with fresh berries, fresh mint and chocolate shavings.

WATER'S EDGE
RESTAURANT & PRIVATE DINING ROOMS

EXECUTIVE CHEF
Ari Nieminen

ICE CREAM STACK

CHOCOLATE COOKIE

11 oz. unsweetened chocolate, chopped
32 oz. semi-sweet chocolate, chopped
4 sticks butter
1 cup all purpose flour
1 ¼ tsp. baking powder
2 ½ tsp. salt
11 eggs
4 cups sugar
2 Tbsp. vanilla
4 cups pecans

1. Melt butter and chocolates in a double boiler or a bowl over a pot of gently simmering water.
2. Sift together the baking powder, flour, and salt.
3. In a separate bowl, whisk the eggs, sugar, and vanilla.
4. Lightly toast the pecans and then chop them.
5. Pour the eggs into the chocolate.
6. Add the flour mix and fold until just blended.
7. Put into a 9" square pan with sides at least 1 ½" high and refrigerate.
8. Once solid, cut into three sections. Take each of these 3" wide sections and cut thin cookies (¼").
9. Bake at 325°, on a parchment lined tray, for 7 minutes.

BANANAS FOSTER

1 cup bananas
4 Tbsp. butter, unsalted
¼ cup brown sugar
2 Tbsp. spiced rum
1 tsp. vanilla extract

1. Take the bananas, peel them, and cut in half. Then cut into quarters lengthwise.
2. In a sauté pan, heat the butter and sugar until the sugar dissolves.
3. Add the bananas and toss gently until they become warmed through and coated.
4. Add rum and vanilla to deglaze.
5. Remove from heat.

ASSEMBLY

Guava ice cream, store bought
Vanilla ice cream, store bought

1. Lay 2 cookies down on a plate and place one small scoop of vanilla and guava ice cream on each cookie.
2. Place 1 of the cookies on top of the other and alternate the ice creams so that the colors stack.
3. Place the top layer of cookie and then spoon on the warm bananas.

Chispa
CORAL GABLES
RESTAURANT BAR℠

EXECUTIVE CHEF
Robbin Haas

CORPORATE CHEF
Adam Botaw

BITTERSWEET CHOCOLATE CAKE WITH PIGNOLI TOFFEE SAUCE AND CHESTNUT ICE CREAM

SERVES 6

CHESTNUT ICE CREAM

YIELDS 1 QUART

1 cup milk

2 cups cream

6 oz. can chestnut puree

¾ cup sugar

8 egg yolks

¼ tsp. salt

2 Tbsp. rum

1. In a heavy bottomed pan, heat the cream, milk, ½ a cup of the sugar, and the chestnut puree. Once the cream begins to boil, remove it from the heat and set aside for 10 minutes. Meanwhile, in a mixing bowl, briskly whisk together the egg yolks, salt, and remaining sugar for 2 minutes. Slowly, using a ladle, whisk some of the hot liquid into the egg mixture to warm it. Gradually pour the warmed egg mixture into the hot milk mixture, whisking the cream constantly as you pour.

2. Cook the custard over medium heat, continuously stirring and scraping the bottom with a rubber spatula or wooden spoon. Remove it from the heat once the custard thickens enough to coat the back of a spoon.

3. Strain the custard through a mesh strainer to remove any lumps of chestnuts. Use the back of the ladle to squeeze through as much cooked chestnut as possible.

4. Chill this chestnut crème anglaise, or ice cream custard base, over an ice bath.

5. Once it is cool, add the rum.

6. Allow the ice cream base to sit in the refrigerator for a minimum of 2 hours and up to 2 days before churning it in an ice cream machine.

7. Churn in an ice cream maker according to the manufacturer's instructions. The ice cream is finished once it has increased in volume and it holds the line of the stirring mechanism. It should mound like softly whipped cream. At this point, you must freeze the ice cream for 4 hours to attain a scoopable consistency.

CHANTERELLE

PASTRY CHEF
Kate Zuckerman

TOFFEE SAUCE

YIELDS 10 OZ.

4 Tbsp. butter

⅓ cup brown sugar

⅓ cup white sugar

1 Tbsp. water

¼ cup corn syrup

¼ cup cream

¼ cup pignoli nuts, toasted and chopped

2 Tbsp. rum

1. In a heavy bottomed saucepot, bring butter, brown sugar, white sugar, water, and corn syrup to a boil. Briskly whisk the sauce once it has come to a boil and then simmer it for 6 minutes. Remove the pot from the heat and allow the caramel to cool for a ½ hour.

2. Once the sauce is cool enough to touch, whisk in the cream, the nuts, and the rum.

3. Serve this sauce warm with the flourless dark chocolate cake.

FLOURLESS CHOCOLATE CAKE

YIELDS 6 INDIVIDUAL CAKES

½ vanilla bean

½ cup water

¾ cup sugar

9 oz. dark chocolate

3 eggs, room temperature

1 egg yolk, room temperature

12 Tbsp. butter, room temperature

1. Preheat the oven to 350º, then grease and sugar 6 ring molds (3" or 4").

3. Run a paring knife down the center of the vanilla bean. Split it open with your fingers and use the knife to scrape out the tiny black seeds into a heavy bottomed saucepan.

4. Add the water, sugar, and vanilla pod and bring to a rolling boil. Remove from heat.

5. Chop the chocolate up into ½" pieces and place them in a medium sized bowl. Pour ½ of the hot vanilla syrup over the chocolate and begin whisking gently. The chocolate will begin to seize a bit. Add the remaining vanilla syrup and continue whisking the chocolate until you have a shiny, thick chocolate sauce, approximately 2 minutes.

6. Add the eggs and yolk, one at a time, whisking after each addition.

7. Next, add the butter, 2 tablespoons at a time. Continue whisking the batter until all the butter has blended into the chocolate. The finished cake batter should be shiny and thick.

8. Scrape the batter into the prepared molds.

9. Bake the cake at 350º for approximately 20 minutes. If the batter is coming out of the refrigerator, allow it to come to room temperature before baking. The cake will rise, crack, and develop a glossy, thin crust on the top. If you gently press down on the center of a cake, it should have a slight spring to it. Remove the cakes and allow them to cool for 1 hour before serving.

Strawberry Melba with Lime Chantilly and Strawberry Sorbet

Serves 8

Strawberry Sorbet

1 ⅔ cup water
1 cup sugar
⅓ cup glucose sugar
2 tsp. stabilizer
4 cups strawberry puree

1. In a small pot, bring the water, sugar, glucose, and stabilizer to a boil over high heat.
2. Whisk in the strawberry puree.
3. Using a hand-held immersion blender, mix until smooth.
4. Transfer to a small bowl and refrigerate.
5. When cool, process in an ice cream maker.

Strawberry Compote

⅓ cup sugar
¼ cup plus 2 Tbsp. water
½ cup strawberry puree
1 ½ lbs. large strawberries, hulled and finely diced
2 vanilla beans, split and scraped

1. In a small saucepan, bring the sugar and water to a boil over high heat.
2. Add the strawberry puree, bring to a boil, and reduce to a simmer.
3. Add the strawberries and vanilla bean seeds and cook for 2 minutes.
4. Transfer the strawberry compote to a small bowl and allow to cool.
5. Cover and refrigerate until needed.

Lime Gelee

7 limes
3 - 2-gram gelatin sheets
⅓ cup plus 2 Tbsp. water
½ cup sugar

1. Finely grate the zest of 2 of the limes and then squeeze enough juice to equal ¾ cup plus 2 tablespoons.
2. Soften the gelatin sheets in a small bowl of cold water for 15 minutes. Lift the gelatin out of the water and squeeze it gently to remove excess moisture.
3. In a small pot, bring the water and sugar to a boil. Remove from the heat and whisk in the lime zest and juice and the softened gelatin sheets.
4. Divide the lime juice mixture among eight 6-ounce glasses.
5. Refrigerate until set.

Lime Whipped Cream

2 Tbsp. sugar
1 cup heavy cream
Finely grated zest of 1 lime
½ vanilla bean, split and scraped

1. Put all the ingredients in a medium bowl.
2. Using a wire whisk or a mixer, whip until medium peaks form.
3. Cover and refrigerate until needed.

CAFÉ BOULUD

NEW YORK • PALM BEACH

Pastry Chef
Eric Bertoia

LINTZER DOUGH

8 oz. (2 sticks) butter
¾ cup sugar
½ tsp. salt
¼ tsp. cinnamon powder
Pinch of nutmeg
½ cup plus 2 Tbsp. hazelnut flour
1 egg
¼ tsp. vanilla extract
1 ¼ cups pastry flour

1. Combine sugar and water in a small saucepan, simmer to dissolve sugar.
2. Add the cranberries and gently cook them for several minutes until they burst.
3. Cool mixture and puree in a food processor.
4. Strain through a fine sieve, saving the liquid, and discarding the solids.
5. Add orange juice, zest, and lemon juice.
6. Chill in a low, flat container in the freezer.
7. After 1 hour or so, scrape granita with a fork. Return to freezer and scrape every ½ hour until you have an evenly textured, flaky product.
8. Reserve in the freezer until you are ready to assemble the dessert.

TO SERVE

Fresh strawberries, sliced

1. Place ¼ cup of compote on top of each gelee.
2. Place a scoop of strawberry sorbet on top of the compote and decoratively circle the ice cream with the whipped cream.
3. Place a lintzer tart on each plate and fan the strawberry slices out across the top of the lintzer decoratively.

Milk Chocolate Hazelnut "Kit Kat Bars"

2 lbs. 4 oz. milk chocolate

15 oz. butter, unsalted

5 lbs. hazelnut paste, unsweetened

1 lb. 3 oz. feuilletine
(available a specialty stores)

1 lb. semi-sweet chocolate

1. Chop the milk chocolate into small chunks and melt with the butter over a double boiler.

2. Fold in the unsweetened hazelnut paste and feuilletine.

3. Pour into a 12 x 18 sheet pan and let cool.

4. Cut into bars.

5. Chop the semi-sweet chocolate into small chunks and melt over a double boiler or in a microwave, in 20 second intervals, stirring after each. Be careful not to overheat.

6. Line a cookie sheet with parchment or wax paper.

7. Dip the bars in the melted semi-sweet chocolate and place on cookie sheet to set.

CHEF ALLEN'S

CHEF/OWNER
Allen Susser

AVENTURA

CARAMEL BANANA BRULEE

Serves 6

CRÈME BRULEE

1 qt. half and half

1 cup sugar

½ vanilla bean, split lengthwise
or 1 Tbsp. vanilla extract

4 eggs

8 egg yolks

1. In a saucepan over medium-high heat, bring the cream, sugar and vanilla bean (if using extract, add at the end) to a boil.
2. In a separate bowl whisk yolks and eggs until liquid. Whisk in boiling milk in a thin stream.
3. Strain through a fine mesh sieve into a bowl and skim foam from surface. Stir in vanilla extract, if used. Spread onto a small sheet pan with sides. Bake at 250° for about 30 minutes, or until firm.

TOASTED ALMONDS

½ cup simple sugar syrup

½ cup blanched, toasted almonds

1 Tbsp. butter, sliced thinly

1. Toss almonds with ½ cup warm syrup in a large bowl.
2. Spread evenly onto a silpat (silicone mat) or a well greased baking sheet.
3. Lay butter pieces on top and bake at 300°, turning frequently until dark golden brown.

NoMI

EXECUTIVE CHEF
Sandro Gamba

CHICAGO

SAUTÉED BANANAS

2 bananas, sliced

1 Tbsp. lemon juice

⅓ cup plus 1 Tbsp. sugar

3 Tbsp. butter, melted

Pinch of powdered ginger

1. Slice the bananas ⅓" thick and toss with lemon juice.
2. In a large Teflon sauté pan, over medium-high heat, cook sugar until it caramelizes to dark amber. Carefully add butter, bananas and lemon juice and swirl around quickly.
3. Add a pinch of ginger and cook quickly until bananas are coated in sauce.
4. Pour back into the bowl to help cool quickly. Set aside.

ALMOND PHYLLO

½ cup sugar

½ cup almond flour

6 Tbsp. clarified butter, melted

3 sheets phyllo dough

1. In a small bowl, blend sugar and almond flour with a whisk.
2. Brush a layer of phyllo with melted butter and sprinkle with almond mixture. Place another phyllo sheet on top and repeat. butter and almond mixture. Repeat with a third phyllo sheet.
3. Put parchment paper on top of phyllo and flatten with rolling pin to adhere layers. Cut 3" x 3" squares.
4. Bake at 325°, covered with parchment and light pan to weigh down the phyllo. Bake for about 10 minutes, until golden.

CARAMEL FOAM

⅓ cup plus 1 Tbsp. sugar

1½ cups cream

1½ cups milk

⅓ vanilla bean

⅔ cup plus 1 Tbsp. sugar

4 egg yolks

1. Caramelize first amount of sugar by placing in a small saucepan over medium-high heat. Move sugar very gently to incorporate with un-dissolved sugar to ensure even cooking. Do not stir. The sugar will caramelize very quickly to a medium-dark amber color.
2. Add cream, milk, and vanilla carefully.
3. In a bowl, mix yolks and second amount of sugar.
4. Add ¼ of the cream caramel mixture to the yolks/sugar mixture, whisking constantly. Return cream caramel mixture to heat and add yolk sugar mixture while whisking. Cook, stirring continuously until it coats the back of a wooden spoon and running your finger over it leaves a line.
5. Immediately strain through a fine mesh strainer into a bowl and place on another bowl filled with ice water.
6. Stir occasionally to cool. When cool, whip with stand or hand mixer on high speed until light and foamy.

GRUE TUILE

12 Tbsp. butter, melted

½ cup and 4 Tbsp. sugar

½ tsp. pectin

4 Tbsp. glucose

4 Tbsp. milk

1 cup Grue de Cacao
or cocoa powder

1. Mix sugar, pectin, and butter. Fold in the glucose, milk, and ½ of the grue di cacao and cook to 110°C. Reserve the rest of the grue for garnish.
2. Pour on a parchment lined cookie sheet, cover with parchment paper and roll thinly.
3. Remove top sheet of parchment paper and bake at 350° for 6 to 8 minutes. Remove from oven and break into pieces.
4. Store in an airtight container.

CHOCOLATE ALMOND CAKE WITH POACHED PEAR

SERVES 12

CHOCOLATE ALMOND CAKE

1 Tbsp. butter
1 cup almond flour
2 Tbsp. cocoa powder
2 egg whites
½ cup sugar
¾ cup bittersweet chocolate, chopped
1 tsp. lemon zest

1. Spray savarin molds with non-stick spray. Dredge with sugar and spray a second time. Set aside.
2. Preheat oven to 350º.
3. Melt butter and set aside.
4. Sift together the almond flour and cocoa into a large bowl.
5. Whisk egg whites until foamy. Add sugar slowly, whisking until stiff.
6. Pour stiff whites onto flour/cocoa mixture. Start to fold mixture together lightly but stop half way.
7. Scoop ¼ of the mixture into the bowl with the melted butter and fold together quickly. Add back to remaining batter and fold together.
8. Use piping bag to fill prepared molds or use a spatula to fill.
9. Bake for 20 to 25 minutes. Remove from oven and cool for 5 minutes before unmolding.

POACHED PEARS

6 small bosc pears
5 cups water
2 ½ cups sugar

1. Combine water and sugar in a 6 quart sauce pan.
2. Wash pears and peel. Place in sugar water. Cover partially.
3. Put over medium heat and bring to a boil, slowly (approximately 15 minutes)
4. Reduce heat and simmer for approximately 20 minutes, until pears are easily pierced with a paring knife.
5. Remove from heat and cool.

PEAR SALAD

Poached pears
Lemon zest
Lemon juice
Poire Williams

1. Cut poached pears in half, leaving stem on one half. Cut the halves that have the stem in half again, cutting the stem in half. Set quarters with stems aside.
2. Clean remaining pear pieces and cut into small dice.
3. Season dice with lemon zest, lemon juice, and Poire Williams.

MILK CHOCOLATE CRÈME ANGLAISE

2 cups half and half
3 Tbsp. sugar
4 egg yolks
4 Tbsp. sugar
3 oz. fine Swiss milk chocolate, chopped fine

1. Bring half and half and first sugar to a boil.
2. Whisk together yolks and second sugar.
3. Pour boiling liquid into yolks in a steady stream while whisking constantly.
4. Return liquid to pot and return to heat and cook while stirring gently with a wooden spoon, until nappe is achieved (a line is formed without blurring edges when finger is run down back of the spoon).
5. Remove from heat and whisk in milk chocolate.
6. Strain and chill.

ASSEMBLY

Pear Sorbet, store bought

1. Reheat cake and place in bottom of a shallow bowl.
2. Circle cake with chocolate crème anglaise.
3. Stand pear quarter in center of cake.
4. Fill center of cake with salad.
5. Top salad with quenelle of pear sorbet.

CAFÉ GRAY
NEW YORK

PASTRY CHEF
Chris Broberg

CHERIMOYA SORBET

6 Cherimoya (fully ripe)
½ cup water
3 Tbsp. sugar
½ cup Baumes de Venise or other dessert wine

1. Peel ripe Cherimoya and remove seeds. Set aside.
2. In a small sauce pan, boil water and sugar over medium. Remove from heat and add Baumes de Venise.
3. Transfer Cherimoya pieces and liquid to a blender.
4. Blend on high until smooth and cool.
5. Freeze in an ice cream maker according to manufacturers directions.
6. Serve right out of the machine for the best flavor and texture.

NOTE FROM THE CHEF

Cherimoya, sometimes called "custard apple" because of it's rich, creamy texture, have become available in the States recently though they have been known for years in South America and Southeast Asia. I can't think of a more luscious and decadent fruit, not counting myself, of course.

They look something like an avocado with armor and, in fact, ripen in much the same way. They should be soft but not mushy to the touch. It is essential to let them fully ripen, somewhat darkened to the skin. They have a soft texture and their fullest complex flavor at this stage and the addition of a little dessert wine to the recipe insures that the sorbet will not become too solid in the freezer and will be easy to scoop.

Cherimoyas are available off and on from May to November and this recipe is rich enough to satisfy the most demanding dessert lover, yet it has no fat at all.

JOSEPHS.
CITARELLA

EXECUTIVE CHEF
Bill Yosses

Granny Smith Apple Tart Tatin with Apple Chips and Lemon Candy Ice Cream

Caramel

1 cup sugar
½ stick of butter

1. In a pan, over medium-high heat, cook the sugar until golden brown.
2. Remove from heat and carefully add the butter.

Tart

10 granny smith apples
4 sticks butter
1 cup sugar
Prepared caramel
Puff pastry, store bought, frozen

1. Peel and cut apples into 8 pieces.
2. Saute them with butter and sugar until they begin to soften and lose some liquid.
3. Pour ¼" of caramel into the bottom of 8 individual 3" tart molds.
4. Arrange apples in the molds, approximately 10 pieces in each.
5. Bake at 280º for 1 hour. Let them rest overnight for best results.

Puff Pastry

2 puff pastry sheets
Prepared caramel

1. Cut 8, 3" disks from the puff pastry sheets. (4 disks per sheet)
2. Place on parchment lined sheet pan and bake at 425º for 7 to 10 minutes, until golden in color.
3. Spread each disk with prepared caramel.
4. Add a disk of caramelized puff pastry to each tart mold and invert.

Citrus Crumbs
TO GARNISH THE PLATE

¼ cup flour
¼ cup fibert flour
⅓ cup sugar
⅓ stick unsalted butter, melted
Zest from ¼ of an orange
Zest from ¼ of a lemon
2 Tbsp. salt

1. Add all dry ingredients in a mixing bowl and mix for a few minutes.
2. Add melted butter.
3. Bake at 300º for 15 minutes.

Lemon Candy Ice Cream

2 cups lemon juice
Zest of 5 lemons
½ cup sugar
12 eggs
1 cup plain yogurt

1. Place all ingredients, except the yogurt, in a double boiler.
2. Whisk while cooking until a custard develops. Let cool off.
3. Mix in the yogurt.
4. Strain, cool and run through an ice cream machine.

Apple Chips

1 granny smith apple, sliced thin
1 cup confectioners' sugar

1. Coat apples with confectioners' sugar.
2. Bake at 200º for 4 hours.

CAFÉ CENTRO

PASTRY CHEF
Phillippe Fallait

TRIPLE GINGER POUNDCAKE

The Institute
of Culinary Education

PASTRY CHEF
Andrea Tutunjian

POUNDCAKE

2 ¼ cups all purpose flour
3 tbsp. ground ginger
¼ tsp. ground cardamom
¼ tsp. baking soda
¼ tsp. salt
1 ½ sticks softened butter
1 ¾ cups granulated sugar, divided
2 oz fresh ginger, peeled and grated
4 eggs, separated
⅔ cup sour cream
½ cup candied ginger, cut into ¼"
pieces divided

1. Preheat the oven to 350°. Butter and line a 9 x 5 x 3-inch loaf pan with parchment or foil.
2. Mix the flour, ground ginger, ground cardamom, baking soda and salt together. Set aside.
3. In a standing mixer, cream the butter with 1 ¼ cups of the sugar until soft, for approximately 2 minutes.
4. Add fresh ginger and continue to beat another minute. Beat in the yolks one at a time, scraping down sides and mixing well after each addition.
5. Add ½ of the dry ingredients mixing until just incorporated. Add all the sour cream, again mixing until incorporated. Finish with the remaining dry ingredients. Stir in half the candied ginger.
6. In a clean dry bowl, whisk egg whites on medium speed until opaque. Gradually add remaining sugar in a steady stream, and whisk until whites hold a soft peak.
7. Gently fold whites into batter. Pour into prepared pan and sprinkle the remaining candied ginger on top.
8. Bake for approximately 80 to 90 minutes, or until an inserted toothpick comes out clean from the center of the loaf.
9. Cool on a rack for 5 or 10 minutes and remove from pan. Allow to complete cooling on a rack.
10. Serve plain or with lemon grass syrup below.

LEMONGRASS SYRUP

1 cup water
1 cup granulated sugar
1 stalk lemongrass, white part only, split
3 strips lemon zest

1. Place water in a sauce pan with all remaining ingredients.
2. Bring to a boil over medium heat, stirring occasionally.
3. Continue to boil for 5 minutes until syrup thickens. Let stand until cooled. Strain and chill until ready to use.

CHOCOLATE BOMBES

GANDUJA GANACHE
(HAZELNUT CHOCOLATE)
8 oz. semi-sweet chocolate
1 lb. Ganduja
(available in specialty stores)
4 Tbsp. butter
¼ cup glucose syrup
3 cups heavy cream

1. Measure into a mixing bowl, all of the ingredients except the heavy cream.
2. In a cooking pot, bring the heavy cream to a boil and then temper with the chocolate mixture, adding gradually. Stir constantly with a spatula until the chocolate dissolves and the mixture is nice and shiny.

DEVILS FOOD CAKE
2 cups cocoa powder
4 cups coffee, fresh brewed
1 lb. (4 sticks) butter
6 cups sugar
8 eggs
6 cups all purpose flour
1 tsp. baking powder
4 tsp. baking soda

1. Mix cocoa powder and coffee together.
2. Cream the butter and sugar and then add in the eggs, one at a time.
3. Sift all the dry ingredients together.
4. Alternate the cocoa powder mixture and the dry ingredients into the butter mixture.
5. Stop the machine and scrape the sides and bottom of the mixing bowl. Then let it run for 2 more minutes.
6. Prepare baking pan with parchment paper at the bottom and spray with non-stick cooking spray.
7. Pour cake batter into baking pan and bake at 300º for 30 minutes.
8. Let it cool and then cut out the circular bombes. They should be 4" in diameter and 1" thick.

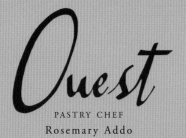

PASTRY CHEF
Rosemary Addo

Frozen Praline Chocolate Mousse

6 cups heavy cream
8 oz. semi-sweet chocolate
20 oz. milk chocolate
12 egg yolks
¾ cup honey
½ cup Frangelico

1. Whip cream until medium peaks and set aside.
2. Melt both chocolates together over a double boiler and leave at room temperature.
3. Boil the honey.
4. Whip the egg yolks to medium peaks and then add in the honey. While the machine is running, add in the Frangelico.
5. Stop the machine and with a spatula, fold the melted chocolate into the egg yolk mixture. Then fold in the whipped cream.
6. Prepare 4" round flexipans and pipe or pour the mousse into the molds.
7. Take one of the devils food cake bombes and cover the top of the mousse with the cake. Freeze for 2 hours.

Ganache

1 ½ cups heavy cream
10 oz good quality dark chocolate

1. Chop chocolate into small pieces.
2. Heat cream in saucepan. When cream boils, remove from heat.
3. Pour over chocolate and beat with a dry spoon until mixed.

Assembly

1. Un-mold the frozen mousse onto a wire rack with a sheet pan under it.
2. Pour the ganache over the un-molded, frozen mousse, tapping the sheet pan gently so that the ganache spreads over the mousse evenly.
3. You can serve with a chocolate tuile and chocolate sauce or serve it just as it is.

CHOCOLATE BERGAMOT TART

PASTRY CHEF
Amanda Labarbera

MAKES 1 – 9 ½-INCH TART

DOUGH
4 oz. unsalted butter, cold and cubed
½ cup confectioners' sugar
2 egg yolks
1 ½ cups all purpose flour
Zest of 1 bergamot

1. In a food processor, blend butter, sugar, and egg yolks.
2. Add flour and zest, pulsing, scraping down the sides as necessary.
3. Blend until dough is moistened and begins forming a ball.
4. Gather dough into a ball and then flatten into a disk.
5. Wrap in plastic and refrigerate for 1 hour (can be made up to 2 days ahead. Keep chilled. Soften lightly at room temperature before rolling).
6. On a lightly floured surface, roll dough into an 11" circle and place into tart pan that has been generously sprayed with non-stick spray.
7. Gently pierce bottom of the tart with a fork in several places and chill for at least 30 minutes before baking.
8. Bake crust at 300° until it begins to color and feels firm to the touch.
9. Prepare filling while crust is baking.

FILLING
1 Tbsp. cornstarch
¾ cup sugar
3 eggs
1 egg yolk
Zest of 1 bergamot
½ cup bergamot juice (you may substitute lemon juice)

1. Stir together cornstarch and sugar.
2. In a stainless steel bowl, whisk eggs, egg yolk, zest, and juice until combined (do not over whisk). Whisk in cornstarch and sugar.
3. Place mixture in a bowl over a pan of simmering water, and heat stirring constantly, until the filling has thickened. (do not over cook).
4. Pour mixture into the tart shell and bake for an additional 5 to 8 minutes or until the filling is completely set.
5. Cool tart.
6. While the filling is baking, prepare the chocolate topping.

CHOCOLATE GANACHE
½ cup cream
4 oz. semisweet chocolate, chopped

1. In a small sauce pan, bring cream to a boil over medium heat.
2. Remove from heat and pour over chocolate.
3. Let sit one minute and then gently stir to melt chocolate.
4. Let cool, stirring occasionally until ganache thickens slightly.
5. Pour over cooled tart.

Lemon Crème Caramel with Blueberry Caramel and Almond Tart, Blueberry Sorbet

Lemon Crème Caramel
3 cups milk
3 cups heavy cream
1 cup sugar
5 eggs
7 egg yolks
Zest of 3 lemons

1. In a heavy bottomed saucepan, bring the milk, cream and lemon zest to a boil and remove from heat.
2. Whisk together the egg yolks, whole eggs and sugar. Slowly add the hot milk mixture to the egg mixture while continuing to whisk until all the milk has been added.
3. Strain the mixture into a clean bowl and chill.
4. Pour into ramekins.
5. Place the ramekins in a water bath (pan of hot water), covered with aluminum foil.
6. Bake at 300º for about 15 minutes or until set.

Frangipane
7 Tbsp. butter
⅓ cup plus 2 Tbsp. almond paste
⅓ cup plus 2 Tbsp. sugar
2 eggs
3 Tbsp. cake flour

1. Cream the butter and almond paste until there are no lumps.
2. Add the sugar and mix until combined.
3. Add the eggs and then the flour and mix until combined.
4. Fill the pre-baked tart shell half way with the frangipane and bake at 350º until set, lightly golden and firm.

Almond Tart Dough
1 egg
4 oz. (1 stick) butter
⅛ rounded cup confectioners' sugar
⅖ cup all purpose flour
3 ½ Tbsp. almond flour

1. Cream together the butter and confectioners sugar until combined.
2. Mix in the egg and then add in the flours and mix until just combined. Do not overmix.
3. Wrap the dough in plastic wrap and refrigerate for an hour.
4. When the dough is chilled, on a lightly floured work surface, roll out to ¼" thick round.
5. To place in tart pan, roll the dough up on the floured rolling pin and unroll over tart pan. Adjust and press/patch where needed.
6. Let rest in freezer for 10 minutes.
7. In a preheated 350º oven, pre-bake the shell until light golden brown, about 15 minutes. Check the dough halfway and press down any bubbles that form.
8. Cool.

Caramel Sauce for Tart
2 cups sugar
½ cup water
2 Tbsp. light corn syrup
¾ cup heavy cream, heated

1. Mix together the sugar, water and corn syrup in heavy bottomed saucepan.
2. Wash down the sides of the pot with a pastry brush dipped in water so there is no sugar clinging to them. Place on high heat and do not touch until mixture begins to caramelize. At this point you can begin to stir the mixture with a wooden spoon and cook to medium amber color.
3. Slowly pour the heated heavy cream very slowly into the caramel stirring to incorporate. When all the cream has been added, let mixture cool at room temperature.

Blueberry, Caramel, Almond Mixture
1 cup blueberries
1 cup almonds, sliced and toasted
Enough caramel to coat mixture

1. Coat blueberry and almonds with the caramel.
2. Place enough of the blueberry mixture on top of the cooked frangipane to make it look full.
3. Bake for 5 minutes longer and remove.
4. Drizzle with some more caramel sauce and serve immediately with the Lemon Crème Caramel.

PASTRY CHEF
Ellen Sternau

The Restaurants

2 WEST
(917) 790-2525
www.ritzcarlton.com

21 CLUB
(212) 582-7200
www.21club.com

ALAIN DUCASSE
(212) 265-7300
www.alain-ducasse.com

ALINEA
(312) 560-6252

ALLEN STREET BAKERY
NEW YORK CITY

AQUAVIT
(212) 307-7311
www.aquavit.org

ART INSTITUTE OF NYC
(800) 654-2433

AUREOLE
(212) 319-1660
www.charliepalmer.com

BAKE
(718) 222-0345
www.bakednyc.com

BEACON
(212) 332-0500
www.beaconnyc.com

BEPPE
(212) 982-8422
www.beppenyc.com

BLUE FIN
(212) 918-1400
www.brguestrestaurants.com

BLUE HILL AT STONE
BARNS
(914) 366-9606
www.bluehillstonebarns.com

BLUE SMOKE
(212) 447-7733
www.bluesmoke.com

BRASSERIE
(212) 751-4840
www.resaurantassociates.com

CAFÉ BOULUD
(212) 772-2600
www.danielnyc.com

CAFÉ CENTRO
(212) 818-1222
www.restaurantassociates.com

CAFÉ GRAY
(212) 823-6338
www.cafegray.com

CASA TUA
(305) 673-1010
www.casatualifestyle.com

'CESCA
(212) 787-6300
www.cescanyc.com

CHANTARELLE
(212) 966-6960
www.chanterellenyc.com

CHEF ALLEN'S
(305) 935-2900
www.chefallen.com

CHISPA
(305)648-2600
www.chisparestaurant.com

CRAFT
(212) 780-0880

DANIEL
(212) 288-0033
www.danielnyc.com

DAVID BURKE &
DONATELLA
(212) 813-2121
www.dbdrestaurant.com

DB BISTRO MODERNE
(212) 391-2400
www.danielnyc.com

DEVI
(212) 691-1300
www.devinyc.com

EMPORIUM BRASIL
(212) 764-4646

FAUCHON
(212) 308-5919
www.fauchon.com

FIREBIRD
(212) 586-0244
www.firebirdrestaurant.com

FLEUR DE SEL
(212) 460-9100
www.fleurdeselnyc.com

FOUR SEASONS HOTEL
(212) 758-5700

FRENCH CULINARY
INSTITUTE
(212) 219-8890

GABY
(212) 782-3040

GONZO
(212) 645-4606

GOOD ENOUGH TO EAT
(212) 496-0163
www.goodenoughtoeat.com

IAN
(212) 861-1993

INSTITUTE OF CULINARY
EDUCATION
(212) 847-0700

JOSEPHS
(212) 332-1515
www.josephscitarella.com

LANDMARC
(212) 343-3883
www.landmarc-restaurant.com

LAYLA
(212) 431-0700

LE BERNARDIN
(212) 554-1515
www.le-bernardin.com

LE ZIE
(212) 206-8686

MARK'S
(954) 463-1000

MAROONS
(212) 206-8640
www.maroonsnyc.com

MARSEILLE
(212) 333-2323
www.marseillenyc.com

METRAZUR
(212) 687-4600
www.charliepalmer.com

MIX
(212) 583-0300
www.chinagrillmgt.com

MR. K'S
(212) 583-1668

NAPLES 45
(212) 972-7001
www.restaurantassociates.com

NEGRIL
(212) 477-2804
www.negrilvillage.com

NOBU
(212) 219-0500
www.myriadrestaurantgroup.com

NOMI
(312) 239-4030
www.nomirestaurant.com

OCEANA
(212) 759-5941
www.oceanarestaurant.com

OTTO
(212) 995-9559
www.ottopizzeria.com

OUEST
(212) 580-8770
www.ouestny.com

OYSTER BAR
(212) 490-6650
www.oysterbarny.com

PLUTON
(312) 266-1440

PULSE
(212) 218-8666
www.myriadrestaurantgroup.com

RIVER CAFÉ
(718) 522-5200
www.rivercafe.com

SANDIA
(212) 627-3700

SEA GRILL
(212) 332-7610
www.restaurantassociates.com

SHAFFER CITY OYSTER
BAR & GRILL
(212) 255-9827

SIAM INN
(212) 757-4006
www.siaminn.com

STRIP HOUSE
www.theglaziergroup.com

SUSHI SAMBA
(212) 475-9377
www.sushisamba.com

TAMARIND
(212) 674-7400
www.tamarinde22.com

TAVERN ON THE GREEN
(212) 873-3200
www.tavernonthegreen.com

THE FOUR SEASONS
(212) 754-9494
www.fourseasonsrestaurant.com

THE MANSION INN
(215) 862-1231
www.themansioninn.com

THE MODERN
(212) 333-1220

TRIBAKERY
(212) 431-0606
www.myriadrestaurantgroup.com

TRU
(312) 202-0001
www.trurestaurant.com

UNION SQUARE CAFÉ
(212) 243-4020

WATER'S EDGE
(718) 482-0033
www.watersedgenyc.com

WD 50
(212) 477-2900
www.wd-50.com